Fast Track Your Sales Team

Hire the Best in the Business

by
Tom Palcheck

Information to Encourage Achievement

1261 West Glenlake
Chicago, IL 60660
www.encouragementpress.com

ISBN-13: 978-1-933766-17-1   ISBN-10: 1-933766-17-4

This product is not intended to provide legal or financial advice or substitute for the advice of an attorney or advisor.

10 9 8 7 6 5 4 3 2 1

©2007, National Institute of Business Management
1750 Old Meadow Road
McClean, VA 22102
www.nibm.net

Introduction, Resources, Index and Appendices
©2007 Encouragement Press, LLC
1261 W. Glenlake
Chicago, IL 60660
www.encouragementpress.com

Fast Track Your Sales Team

Hire the Best in the Business

About the Author

Tom Palcheck is a sales and marketing leader with more than 20 years experience. Starting as a marketing manager and ultimately becoming sales manager, Mr. Palcheck has recruited, hired and trained hundreds of salespeople for a number of consumer product companies. He has spent his career selling directly to a variety of big box stores in the United States, Mexico and Canada–some of the toughest business-to-business customers there are!

Table of Contents

Introduction

Finding, motivating and retaining a top-notch sales team can be a manager's nightmare–unless you have a plan and a well defined set of goals and objectives. Superior managers know that building a great sales team is both art and science. First and foremost, you have to hire the right people for the job–sales pros who are savvy, smart and willing to work. Secondly, you have to keep them sharp, on target and on topic.

Experience tells you that these are not easy tasks. There is a great deal of competition for quality sales personnel; everyone is looking to build a great team. Secondly, you are faced with the obvious need to keep the payroll and bonuses within budget–not to mention the costs for incentives, travel, training and long-term compensation. This is a very delicate balancing act.

As a sales manager (or future sales manager) you have the good sense to realize that just because you have hired the right people, your job does not end there. In fact, it is just beginning. Training and motivation are keys to keeping these great performers at the top of their game.

As the team leader, you must help your salespeople go after the difficult customers–the ones that like to negotiate hard on price or delivery; the big accounts you never seem to land and the accounts that like to listen and be entertained, but never buy. It takes creativity and leadership to help your team achieve and surpass their quotas for the year.

Having been in sales for over 20 years, I understand the problems you face. In this very readable and practical book, I will show you how to sell your company and your sales team to recruit the best in the industry. I will explain the importance of:

- How to target recruiting ads to attract the right candidates.
- Why it is essential to prepare carefully for each interview.
- What questions you can and cannot ask candidates.
- Why hiring a personality is so important.
- Hiring from the competition—a good idea or a bad idea?
- Why helping your people have instant credibility when they sell is so important.
- Having ground rules for joint sales calls.
- Getting the maximum out of an incentive program.
- Handling objections.
- And much, much more…

Sales recruiting, hiring and management are fluid and fast-paced. What always worked in the past is not going to cut it in today's competitive environment. You want the best for your sales team and you want people to be around in years to come so that you are not constantly on the hunt for new team members.

Learn to hire the best: Find the movers and shakers in sales and keep them happy and motivated. Challenge your management approach: Throw out the old and replace it with a fresh, successful and vibrant sales management style which will guarantee success for you and for your team.

Recruit smart and hire the best in the business!

Tom Palcheck

Recruiting & Retaining the Best

The best way to support a successful and dynamic sales force is to implement the right policies in recruitment and compensation. In fact, how you handle these practices creates the foundation on which the quality and success of your sales force are built. By following the appropriate guidelines, you can attract and choose the right salespeople, protect your company legally during the hiring stage and ensure that you do not overpay your salespeople or lose them to competitors because of an unfair compensation/bonus package.

You Are the Key to a Successful Hire

In today's job market, candidates make a big effort to put their best foot forward. They hire professionals to help them write resumés; they read books on how to interview well. As the hiring manager, you need to be at least equally prepared if you want to find the best candidate. Focus on these areas:

The Job

How long is your sales process? Does the unfilled territory call for maintenance, rebuilding or missionary work? What qualities do your successful salespeople have? Use your answers to write your recruitment ad. Try to isolate specifics so that you can ask your candidates pointed questions.

The Interview

Based on your years of selling, you can wing a sales call if you have to. But do not try to wing interviews with job candidates, no matter how many you have conducted. Dissect the candidate's resumé. Have a checklist ready listing essential experience and educational requirements, so you can easily compare resumés to your selection criteria. Pinpoint the areas you want to know more about. Since you will likely be interviewing several candidates, jot down not only the questions you want to ask all of them but the specific questions you have for each.

Ask just enough open-ended questions to keep the information flowing. Fill candidates in on the job duties, but let them do most of the talking. Many experts suggest that you conduct long interviews, say, 2 or 3 hours in duration. The reason: It is a lot harder for candidates to misrepresent themselves when you interview them in depth. For example, say a candidate's resumé claims she turned around a territory. Ask about her company's products or services, the territory's history, what steps the candidate took, her reporting relationships and so on. If she is stretching the truth, you will spot it through her lack of knowledge or discrepancies in her statements. Take notes as you talk so that you can easily compare the candidates and your reactions to them after you have met them all.

One familiar tactic used when interviewing salespeople is to point out an item in the room and have the person deliver a sales pitch for it. Because this is a frequently employed interviewing technique in sales, many recruits are ready for the challenge. But some managers believe that putting a candidate on the spot in this way is unfair. In that case, a better approach might be to ask an applicant to deliver a sales pitch that worked well for him in the past.

Note

Remember that you are the buyer during preliminary job interviews. You do not become a seller of the job until you know you have a candidate you want to hire. Even then, you do not want to push. If you have to do a lot of selling, the candidate probably is not the right person for the job.

The Hire

Before making an offer, always ask for references and make those calls. At the very least, you will confirm employment or education, especially if this is the candidate's first job out of school. With luck, you will also be able to confirm the candidate's claims and get a better fix on her skills.

Checking Background Information

Falsification of credentials is common. Every applicant who submits a resumé wants to attract your attention by presenting his best skills and experience. There is, in all resumés, a degree of persuasive marketing, the ability to explain a candidate's skills in light of the sales position being sought and an active effort to show why he or she is the best candidate.

Observation

Hiring costs you time and money—more than you may think. Do not waste the investment by having lax hiring procedures.

Misstating information can be unintentional; for example, listing an incorrect date or job title in a resumé. It can also be quite intentional, meaning that the applicant will use any means possible to improve his or her chances of landing the sale position. Even among those who misrepresent the facts, there can be extremes: from the proverbial white lie (e.g., enhanced salary) to gross misrepresentation (e.g., claming an advanced degree which was never earned).

Lying on resumés is apparently on the rise. According to a Knight-Ridder-Tribune Business News article, an online survey conducted by the Society for Human Resource Management determined that more than 60 percent of human resource professionals found inaccuracies on resumés. In another online survey, conducted by Korn/Ferry, nearly half the respondents said they believed resumé fraud among executives is increasing.

Is misrepresenting one's qualifications marketing or downright deception? Is there a difference? Do you, as a sales manager, care about this kind of activity? Do you dismiss it, assuming that everyone exaggerates in some way? Where do you draw the line between creative marketing and fraud? Some individuals unnecessarily exaggerate their qualifications. For instance, a high-profile football coach was offered a job in a prestigious college football program; he ultimately resigned after college administrators learned that he claimed an advanced degree that he never earned. He was not hired for this degree, but rather his 20 years of successful teams and coaching. Why the need to embellish when the job was his? There seemingly is a compulsion on the part of even highly successful individuals to cover some flaw, real or imagined.

More pragmatically, most lying on resumés reflects the competitive job market, especially for prime sales positions with successful, reputable companies. Because many employers never go beyond the resumé in rejecting employees, candidates do not have an opportunity to sell themselves in any other way. If an applicant does not make a good first impression on paper, he or she will never even get to the interview stage.

What are some of the typical misrepresentations? Consider some of the responses to that question from employment experts:

- Length of sales experience.

- Misrepresenting accomplishments, exceeding quotas, that sort of thing.

- Reasons for leaving a previous job (which should not be in a resumé in the first place).

- Exaggerating salary and bonuses, knowing that it is difficult to prove otherwise.

- Changing employment dates to cover a period of unemployment.

Applicants often justify these kinds of misrepresentations because they assume that everyone else is overstating accomplishments. Prospective employees worry that not having a certain degree or the exact experience that companies seek means that they will not be offered an interview, much less a job. Experts and professionals who advise job applicants urge people not to lie on resumés and not to exaggerate the facts. It is a simple matter for an employee to verify whether an applicant earned his or her stated degree.

If you want to find out if an applicant is reasonably honest, this is the information to verify. Although Title VII of the Civil Rights Act of 1964 limits the questions you can ask job applicants, it is legal to check public records to verify a candidate's credentials. Potential sources include educational institutions, academic records, driving records, criminal records, workers' compensation claims and even credit histories. Even credit checks? Yes. Although many employers run credit checks on applicants who will be handling money or conducting unsupervised financial transactions with customers, experts say you routinely should include other types of workers.

"Companies that hire lots of entry-level workers can incur a large expense in checking applicants' criminal records and past credit," says Paula Lee, project manager at Transportation Information Services Inc., publisher of *The Guide to Background Investigations*. "But in these types of jobs, there is lots of turnover and plenty of opportunities for security problems."

The basic credit report–which contains data on outstanding debts–is easy to order from a credit bureau and does not require you to obtain the applicant's permission. If you need more detailed information on an applicant's credit history, you can obtain an investigative credit report from a credit agency. These reports delve into a subject's character and include interviews with friends and business associates. The federal Fair Credit Reporting Act requires employers who request investigative credit reports to inform applicants in writing within 3 days. The applicant also can get a copy of the report.

Top Reference-Checking Questions

Having a list of references will not do you any good if you cannot get them to open up to you. If you do not know where to start, try these questions for starters:

- Is this person eligible to be rehired? If not, is this because your company has a general policy on rehiring employees or is there another reason?
- Would you enthusiastically recommend him?
- How would you compare her work habits with those of her co-workers?
- What do you think would be the ideal job for this person?
- Did this person function better at your company working alone or as part of a team?
- What, if anything, distinguishes him from others who do the same type of job?
- What can we expect from her if she works for us?
- What were his primary job responsibilities?
- During the course of her employment at your company, were you her direct supervisor the entire time? If not, who were the other supervisors?

TARGET YOUR RECRUITING ADS—ONLINE AND PRINT

In recent years, online recruitment has grown to become commonplace across the entire employment spectrum. Estimates today suggest that online recruitment is the hiring method of choice for most sales positions. Online recruitment enables a sales manager to capitalize on her company's industry reputation and make its presence known to a wider range of job seekers. A corporate Website is a great vehicle for providing information about the company, its culture and environment and employment opportunities.

Online recruitment not only makes it easy for job seekers to apply for positions, but it also enables companies to easily sift through a large number of applications. Software is also available to facilitate the sorting process. The software scores completed online applications against a model to determine if any meet the position's minimum qualifications. Screening software may not be cost-effective for smaller businesses, however. Manual screening is still useful, but keep in mind that you may have many applications to screen if you are viewed as an employer of choice in your industry.

Here are some tips for reaching applicants online:

1. **Know the criteria for screening.**
   Some online search engines allow you to sort by skill set and geographical location and you can further refine your results by job requirements and applicants' zip codes. The more detailed your search, the more qualified applicants you will find. Online job boards are useful for finding suitable sales candidates, as the posting are directed specifically to selling.

2. **Use the full range of Internet options.**
   Post job listings on popular career websites such as Monster.com, Hotjobs.com and CareerBuilder.com. These sites are frequently a first stop for applicants who use key words to search for opportunities that interest them. There are also industry-specific career sites that target candidates for more specialized positions, for example if you are looking for a sales person for medical devices or high-technology.

3. **Do not waste time; rapid response is best.**
   Many sales managers may be reviewing the same applicant's credentials at the same time, so your best approach is a quick response. There is little time to engage in a lengthy review process. Competition for qualified

applicants is fierce, especially for those positions that require uncommon skill sets. These individuals may post their resumé one week and be gone the next. If you can efficiently identify good candidates, interview and screen them and make offers quickly, you will get the top talent that you need.

So, here are some of the advantages of online sales recruitment:

- **Cost:**
  Internet advertising is significantly less expensive than more traditional advertising methods–perhaps as much as 75 percent less.

- **Time:**
  Employer surveys suggest that online applications and screening have cut the length of the typical hiring cycle in half.

- **Administration:**
  Electronic information storage, whether in-house or online, reduces paper usage and the time and space required to file that information.

But, of course, there are disadvantages as well:

- **Volume:**
  One online job posting can generate a considerable number of resumés to review and sort.

- **Qualifications:**
  Many applicants may not fit the basic qualifications for your sales position.

- **Reach:**
  Not all candidates are comfortable distributing personal information on the Internet. This may leave you with a narrow talent pool if you rely solely on online recruitment.

Not everyone is hired via the Internet; many companies complement their online efforts with traditional advertisements in newspapers, professional journals or other print media. (Some newspapers have relationships with the larger online employment Websites, so you may be able to work out a deal to post your sales positions using both media.)

The way your ad is written can work as a screening tool itself. It can help ensure that the people who respond are likely candidates for the openings you have:

Determine your most effective key word. Most newspapers run employment ads alphabetically according to the first word in the job description headline. But not all sales-oriented positions should begin with the word, Sales. Think about the kind of person you are really looking to hire. For example, if you want a technical person to train as a sales person, you might want the headline to read, Engineer or Chemist. Of course, if you are looking for someone with experience, not a trainee, then Sales would be the appropriate header to use.

Sell the right candidates on your job. The more information you include in your ad, the less time you will have to spend fielding inquiries and the more serious and qualified your applicants are likely to be. Include such basics as these: What the recruit will be selling, type and amount of experience desired, salary or compensation plan, work hours, amount of travel required and some reference to benefits, if applicable. "I advise advertisers to write a product ad," says the employment advertising manager for a major metropolitan newspaper. "Do not just say, I have a job opening. Point out why someone would want it." That way, you will attract the people who want not just any job, but the position you need to fill. The advertising manager also suggests that you track your ads to see what works best for you.

Do not forget to close. Tell applicants how you want them to respond to your ad. You may or may not want to include your company name or the name and number of an individual to contact. If your company is well known, its reputation can be a definite asset in recruitment. On the flip side, you may have reasons for not wanting to alert your employees–or your competitors–that you are hiring. In general, ads for higher-salaried jobs include a box number or a blind e-mail address, rather than a name. This can cut the response rate by as much as 40 percent, but usually the respondents are of a higher caliber.

Do not be too concerned about the size of the ad or the day of the week that it runs. Neither of those factors has been shown to have much bearing on response. "I have seen three-line ads succeed and full-page ads fail," the employment advertising manager says. "The content is what really makes the difference." That is why it is so important to choose your words carefully. It is true that Sunday's ads get the most exposure–not only do they have a larger circulation than weekday papers, but also people have more time to read them. But someone who is seriously seeking a job will be looking at the want ads every day of the week.

Run your ad for several consecutive days. Four to 7 is the recommended number. And remember that the more experience or expertise you require, the longer you will need to run the ad so as to attract an adequate number of qualified applicants.

Recommendation

Consider enlisting the advice of newspaper advertising reps in your recruitment effort. They are trained to help you create ads that work.

POLISH YOUR INTERVIEWING SKILLS

Recruiting and training a sales person involves an enormous investment of time and money. Your goal, of course, is to realize a substantial return on that investment by selecting a person who will turn out to be a solid producer. You can improve the chances of realizing such a return by polishing your own interviewing skills. Keep these tips in mind:

1. **Be precise about your needs.**

   Too often, managers have a feel for the kind of sales person they want. If their intuition fails them, they find out only when the sales person fails. Rather than relying solely on your instinct, write out a description of the job, including every task and ability it requires, day in and day out. Then examine the job description and list the specific skills and qualities an applicant will need to be considered for the opening. For example, part of the description might read: Calls on top human resources executives. One specific skill required to perform that task might be: A working knowledge of the language of behavioral scientists. That is a concrete skill that instinct might miss and it is only one of the many needed to call on that market.

Job Descriptions

Why are job descriptions so important? Providing a written job description for every sales position in your company establishes clear expectations about tasks and responsibilities and eliminates duplication of effort.

A job description typically outlines the necessary skills, training and education needed by a potential employee and lists a job's duties and responsibilities. It can provide an objective basis for interviewing candidates, orienting a new salespeople and evaluating their performance in the field. A well-designed job description simplifies the interview process and informs candidates of a job's requirements. If you know what skills you are looking for, you will have an easier time knowing what questions to ask and identifying which candidates will best fit your open position.

Every job description should include the following:

1. Job title.

2. Job location.

3. Whether the position is exempt or nonexempt according to the Fair Labor Standards Act (FLSA).

4. Financial responsibilities and implications stated in dollars.

5. Summary describing the purpose of the job and why it exists.

6. Listing of specific duties and major responsibilities.

7. Job qualifications, describing the minimum education, experience and skills necessary to perform the job.

8. A general statement of duties and to whom the employee would report.

9. Job functions, including daily tasks and any supervisory functions.

10. Attributes needed for the position. Detail any technical or educational requirements that may be critical or desired.

11. Provide details on the reporting and organizational structure. Include the titles of both the immediate supervisor and any direct reports.

12. Define evaluation criteria.

13. Include the range or grade of compensation rather than a specific figure.

The job description should be free from judgments about how well the job is currently performed or what is expected in the future. It may be used as a tool for measuring and establishing further career development, but these items are better addressed in an sales person's performance review. Job requirements should be tied directly to job demands. Stay objective and nonjudgmental and never define job specifications with a specific individual in mind. Lastly, understand the difference between a job specification and a job description. A job specification identifies the skills and abilities needed to perform a job, while a job description defines the position and describes the job.

2. Plan your questions.

It will take a series of questions to elicit what you need to know about the person. Unless you have a written list of what you want to cover, you are likely to miss something important. Refer to your list and jot down points in the candidate's remarks that you want to remember. Do not worry that your writing will make the candidate nervous. It may, of course. But it will also show her that you are paying attention and are interested. And it is the only way you will be able to remember the relevant details.

3. Give the person room to expand.

Questions that can be answered with a yes or a no will give you answers that the candidate thinks you want to hear–and usually his guess will be correct. But you will learn little about the way the person operates. So do no ask, for example: Have you had any experience in talking to executives of small companies? The response is likely to be yes or even yes, a lot. Instead, say: Tell me how you respond to small-company executives who say, That sounds OK, but I do not think we need it here. Ask for examples of how the person handled a variety of situations; you will learn a lot about the way he can be expected to deal with similar situations for your company.

4. Do not make snap judgments.

This is often an intuition-related error. An applicant says something that either turns on or puts off the manager and that is it. The manager may not even realize it, but from that point on, it is only a pro forma interview. The person is out or in and subjects that might well have reversed the decision are left unexplored. If you catch yourself reacting that way–and you will feel it physically–try to set the feeling aside as you proceed with the interview. Remember that you must consider the whole person as a package. If you let yourself be swayed by one component, you are the one who stands to lose.

5. Stash your closing skills.

Sales managers never lose their flair for making a sale. But it is a misplaced skill in an interview. Early on, give the applicant a summary of the job's requirements. Then listen to the responses. In the end, it is the candidate who must sell you. Avoid closing him–or yourself–on buying the job.

QUESTIONS YOU CAN AND CANNOT ASK APPLICANTS

Interviewing sales candidates in today's regulatory environment is a bit like walking a tightrope. Ask a candidate a forbidden question in the job interview and you can end up in court. But if you fail to ask questions that give you insight into a candidate's ability and motivation to sell and manage a territory, you can end up with a recruit who brings down your region's results and has to be replaced.

Gone are the days when you could simply hire (or fire) someone as you saw fit. You become vulnerable to charges of unfair and illegal personnel practices from the moment you decide to fill a vacancy. The way you draft a job description, advertise the position, interview candidates and select a finalist must conform to a variety of anti-discrimination laws.

Under Title VII of the Civil Rights Act, it is illegal for an employer to discriminate against applicants on the basis of race, color, religion, gender or national origin. Other laws further protect applicants and place more of a burden on you to ensure that your hiring practices are not (intentionally or unintentionally) discriminatory.

Make sure that your questions to applicants request only job-related information that will help you in the selection process. The Americans with Disabilities Act (ADA) flatly prohibits certain questions during initial job interviews. To make sure that you do not end up in court, review the following before your next round of interviews.

THE BASICS

Before making a job offer, the ADA bans any question that is likely to elicit information about a specific disability, but it allows questions about the person's ability to perform the essential functions of the job. The test is whether the question can reasonably be expected to lead to disclosure of a disability.

The distinction can be very subtle, so the Equal Employment Opportunity Commission (EEOC), which enforces the ADA, has adopted an enforcement guidance for its field staff spelling out which questions are permissible and which are not. You are on safe ground if you follow the wording of the allowable questions and you will be almost as safe if you apply its reasoning to the questions you want to ask.

Example

You can ask: How well can you handle stress? But you cannot ask: Have you ever been unable to cope with job-related stress? The reasoning: A lot of people who cannot handle stress well do not have disabilities, but asking about specific past troubles is likely to elicit information as to whether an applicant has a substantially limiting psychological impairment, according to the Equal Employment Opportunity Commission (EEOC). You can also list the various tasks the job entails and ask if the candidate can perform those tasks.

APPROVED AND FORBIDDEN QUESTIONS

Here is a partial list of what you can and cannot ask:

Questions about Obvious Impairments

OK: How did you break your arm?

No: When will it be healed?

OK: Explain or show me how a one-legged person could do the job of a telephone lineman.

No: Explain or show me how a one-legged person could do the job of a telemarketing representative.

Questions about Drug Use

OK: Are you currently using illegal drugs?

No: Have you ever been treated for drug abuse?

No: Have you ever been addicted to drugs?

Questions about Attendance Records

OK: How many days were you absent from work last year?

OK: How many Mondays and Fridays were you absent last year on leave other than approved vacation leave?

No: How many days were you sick last year?

No: How often will you require leave for treatment of your disability?

Questions about Lifestyle

OK: Have you ever been convicted of driving while intoxicated?

No: How much alcohol do you drink each week?

No: Have you ever been treated for alcoholism?

Questions about Accommodations

OK: Our salespeople are required to spend 3 weeks out of every 4 on the road, driving from account to account. They must carry a sample bag that weighs 60 pounds and communicate with the home office via laptop computer. They must also be able to make appointments and service accounts by telephone. Can you perform these functions with or without reasonable accommodation?

No: Would you need reasonable accommodation to perform this job?

Questions about Workers' Compensation Claims History

No inquiries are allowed.

PRE-OFFER VERSUS POST-OFFER

Prohibited questions are forbidden only before you make a bona fide job offer. Once you offer the candidate a job, contingent on the person's fitness to perform it, you can make further inquiries to be sure that the person can do the job. If he cannot, you can legally withdraw your offer. For example, you could withdraw the offer if a post-offer psychological test revealed a tendency toward violent behavior. Ditto if you found the candidate had a history of taking many days of sick leave, one day at a time and daily attendance is vital to performing the job. You can make a job offer conditional on the results of a medical examination or inquiry; if you use medical examinations, however, you must require them of all applicants for that position and there must be a business necessity–you just cannot decide to test because you want to.

Will Your Hiring Practices Pass the Testers?

Managers should be alert to the increased federal use of testers to uncover signs of racial or other bias in hiring practices. In a typical case, two testers present similar credentials when applying for an advertised job. If the job goes, say, to a white applicant instead of to a black one, then alarm bells ring.

The information is passed on to the Equal Employment Opportunity Commission or a state agency for legal action. In a Boston case, a Brooks Brothers store settled for an undisclosed sum after being cited by testers. Out-of-court settlements have also been reached in Florida and California.

A private group called the Fair Employment Council (FEC) is the main sponsor of these probes. It recruits and trains testers in Washington, D.C. and advises groups that test across the nation. Although the EEOC does not finance such operations, it does investigate charges referred to it by the FEC.

Hire Only Clones and You May Sell Yourself Short

We have all seen variations on the cartoon in which a personnel director says to someone who is his mirror image: "I like the cut of your jib." It is tempting to hire people who are much like ourselves; we are more comfortable with them. But it is often not the best approach. Sales managers who reject selling styles or personalities that are different from their own may, in fact, be selling themselves short.

If you have been using yourself as the unvarying standard against which you measure all applicants for your sales team, here are reasons to reconsider doing so:

Recommendation

Do not let the threat of a visit by a tester prevent you from hiring the person you think is right for the job. But do be ready to demonstrate that your decision makes objective sense—that one person has the skills and type of personality you need in sales and the other does not. Some testing groups also are sending in resumés to check responses by employers. Again, it is wise to be prepared to defend your selection criteria and this is further justification for taking the time and effort to write specific job descriptions for each sales team member.

- **There just are not enough clones of you to go around.**

  Good salespeople are hard to find; you are compounding the problem for yourself by insisting on hiring clones. You have certainly met people from whom you would never buy but who somehow sell up a storm. Apparently there are people who will buy from them; they are good at what they do. As one marketing director says: "We have several people in our organization who have demonstrated high levels of success in spite of their poor judgment in not doing things the way I would do them." That is tongue-in-cheek and very much to the point.

- **You may be buying a mirage.**

  Some job interviewees have the ability to figure out from the clues you give–perhaps unknowingly–what characteristics you are seeking. That is what they reflect back to you. First thing you know, you are thinking: I like this person! The danger is that he may do a lot better in interviews than on the job.

Observation

This is not to suggest that there is anything wrong with your style. You may, in fact, be the best. So it is probably inevitable and certainly not inappropriate, to look for people like yourself. Just keep in mind that there are other ways to succeed. And think about how boring it would be if we all were the same.

- **Learning never ends.**

  Yours certainly does not. Otherwise, you would not be where you are. Consider what you know now about things you knew little or nothing about a few years ago: Teleconferencing, perhaps, computers, JIT manufacturing, robots or automated purchasing. Are not some of them new entries in your personal book of knowledge? Says one general manager, "Adding to your staff someone who does things differently from you can be a learning experience all around. Maybe he can take you in a new direction."

DOES THE APPLICANT HAVE THE RIGHT ATTITUDE?

A negative attitude can undermine sales and satisfaction. For five fairly common types of salespeople, a healthy hookup with selling is just out of reach. All five have roadblocks built into their thinking that prevent them from getting out of selling all that selling has to offer. While an applicant may not fit neatly into any of the following profiles, there is a chance that elements of them may become apparent during the job interview. Probe deeply during your interviews with applicants to determine their attitude toward selling. As you review each profile below, consider to what extent, if any, the roadblocks may affect the applicant's success and enjoyment.

The Nonbeliever

This representative has all the makings of a top producer—intelligence, technical proficiency and good product knowledge. But he has a flaw that relegates him to middle-of-the-pack status: He does not believe in his product or service and cannot get excited about selling it. He is aware of his indifference; yet he cannot reconcile his so-so record with the fact that he would not buy the product he sells.

It is a mystery to this person that so many of his colleagues outsell him. He knows that he is as sincere, knowledgeable and hard-working as any of them and he is convinced that if you are smart and trained, which he is, you should be able to go out and do a job. Trouble is, he makes calls, delivers information, talks sense and is pleasant to all without heat. The men and women who outpace the nonbeliever have an enthusiasm for what they do that he cannot match. They are sold on what they sell and he is not and customers can tell the difference. Some customers do not mind a nonbeliever—those are the people this sales person has for accounts. But he cannot sell others. The mediocre job he does frustrates him and prevents him from enjoying his work.

The nonbeliever has two choices: Drop what he is doing and find something he can get fired up about, or get fired up about what he is doing. To do the latter, he must make thorough comparisons between his company and others, between his products and others and between the sum of his product's benefits and others. If his are as good or better, that is all the evidence he would need to transform his state of mind and put some honest heat and joy into selling. Remember, no one says a person has to be a user of a product to sell it. All that is required is a strong belief that users will gain from it.

The Square Peg

This representative has usually worked for a number of firms and sold a variety of products. But none of those jobs has worked out. No matter where she works, this sales rep never feels comfortable—the classic square-peg, round-hole dilemma. Still, she firmly believes that it is not her fault.

One reason the square peg never fits is that she is forever looking for something that is not there. With one company, she finds the product inferior; with another, the customers snobby; with yet another, she considers the operation cheap. Because of her attitude, her sales efforts tend to be superficial. They will improve, she believes, when she finds the ideal situation. She would not, of course, because there are few ideal situations. Those that are ideal are made, not found. The square peg would love to love what she is doing. But instead of working at it, she just keeps searching for it. She will not fit in anywhere until she stops fooling herself and starts using her sales skills to make sales.

The challenge for the square peg: To face the reality that no situation is ideal. Some drawbacks are built into every one of them. If she comes to terms with that, she can then capitalize on opportunities–blemishes and all. She must stop pretending that her lack of success in selling is the fault of other people or events.

The Mad Closer

This representative brings in sales by the bushel-full and then antagonizes or loses many of his customers. He is a closer with a capital C, the kind sales managers dream about–until the complaints and cancellations come rolling in.

Mad closers believe that selling is intended to be–dog eat dog and every man for himself. They think they owe their success to a negative state of mind that allows them to treat customers as pawns. Thus, to enjoy selling is to stop selling because to the mad closer, closing is selling. He will do anything to get the customer's signature on the dotted line, regardless of the consequences. The customer cannot pay for it? Sell it anyway. The product is not what the customer needs? Push it anyway. Have to stretch a point or a promise to make the sale? Do it.

A mad closer can cause more trouble for his company than his sales are worth. And that is a shame because this person has everything it takes to be first rate–desire, talent and energy. Yet it all is misdirected.

The mad closer should try to recognize that he could make more money with less trouble. He could enjoy his career and keep the sales he closes if he would:

- Stop treating each sale as an isolated event.

- Sell the customer what is good for him.

- Make himself indispensable and not reprehensible to his customer and his company by selling clearly and responsibly.

Most mad closers lack the confidence to work from a positive state of mind, which is unfortunate because that is the only way to achieve genuine success.

The Reluctant Closer

This representative likes the excitement of selling, meeting new people, lunching with customers, attending sales functions, even handing out business cards. Her prospect list is enormous, her activity reports legendary. She does everything but write orders because her idea of sales does not include selling. Her idea of sales is being a goodwill ambassador for her company.

The reluctant closer wants to be liked, not rejected. She hates to hear the word no from a customer; that would break up what she had hoped would be a friendship. Thus she is afraid to risk asking for the order. What little business she writes is handed to her.

The reluctant closer should stop playing at selling and treat the social side of it as an extra, not the main event. She should abandon the role of promising rookie and steel herself to accept losses; she would not achieve wins without them.

The Self-Anointed

This representative is a top producer and has no qualms about hammering home that point to all those around him. He has crowned himself king and plays out the role:

- He shares nothing with peers, his manager or other company departments. He refuses to participate in sales meetings and attends as few as possible, denying his colleagues information that might be helpful.

- He ignores new sales techniques and ideas. He points to his record as proof that nothing new is necessary for his continued success. He knows best and anything different is a waste of time.

- He is seldom satisfied with support people. He never says please or thank you and is quick to complain to management about perceived flaws in their performance.

- He complains about not being appreciated, of unfair treatment and of neglect–despite the recognition he regularly earns and is awarded. What he wants is special consideration–for example, his deliveries to be given priority over those of other salespeople.

Self-anointed salespeople can often stay psyched and enjoy what they do for a long period of time. Their smugness and rejection of new thinking, however, generally catch up with them in the long run.

Those who recognize a touch of the self-anointed in themselves should try to open their minds to new thinking. They should make it a game: See how many new ideas or approaches they can collect in a week or month and then make themselves try one of them.

Should You Hire a Competitor's Sales Person?

Know the appropriate answer to that question before you receive the first application from a sales person currently employed, or recently dismissed, by one of your competitors. If movement from one company to another is common among salespeople in your industry, you are probably on firm legal ground. But if the practice is not common:

Memo

If movement is common in your industry and you find your own people job-hopping frequently, rethink your firm's training and compensation practices. Perhaps some changes could be made that would improve your retention rates.

- The former employer may hit you with a lawsuit for stealing trade secrets, such as customer lists and proprietary product information.

- If that should happen, you not only might have to spend time and money defending your case but also might have to disclose some of your firm's trade secrets in the discovery process.

- You may lay yourself open to counter-recruitment efforts.

How Many People Do You Really Need in the Field?

You can calculate the number of sales reps you need for maximum effectiveness if you know what it takes for your average representative to do the job. Here is the formula:

1. **Assign values to customers.**
   Rate each customer and targeted prospect in your area based on call frequency value. For example, an A rating might be worth two calls per month; B, one a month; C, one every 6 weeks and so forth.

2. **Calculate the total number of calls to be made each year.**
   Say you have 100 A accounts at 24 calls a year, 225 B accounts at 12 per year and 200 C accounts at 9 per year. That adds up to 6,900 calls.

3. **Divide by your average daily call rate.**
   Say your people make an average of four calls a day. With 6,900 calls to make, you would need 1,725 sales person days. (Be realistic when determining an average call rate; your people need time for prospecting, paperwork, service calls and so on.)

4. **Divide by 180 working days per person per year.**
   That allows for holidays, sick days, vacations, meetings and so on. Then 1,725 divided by 180 equals 9.58, or 10 salespeople.

Compare this ideal number to the number of representatives you have. If you are covering the territory with significantly more or fewer representatives, do a round of field travel with your people. Perhaps you over- or underestimated the daily call rate (see No. 3 above). Or the addition or subtraction of a product line may have affected the average duration of a sales call.

Recommendation

Do not make immediate drastic changes in the number of salespeople in your group as a result of this calculation. Instead, adjust gradually. You want to protect your people's earnings as well as your sales volume.

Help Recruits Handle the Long and Short of It

Salespeople can often transfer from one industry to another with little difficulty. The product or service may be different, but the selling skills are the same. It is more complicated, however, when a sales person experienced in long-term selling shifts to short-term selling, or vice versa.

Those who enjoy selling big-ticket items or service contracts thrive on the challenge and the big payoff when a sale is made. Those who sell less expensive goods and services are spurred by the constant feedback that a daily closing provides.

Because so many companies are trimming their forces, some salespeople may feel that they must shift from one mode to another, regardless of their preferences. If you can help them adapt to the new pace, you may be able to pick up some top-notch sales talent. Following are some tips.

FROM SHORT-TERM TO LONG-TERM SELLING

This is the more difficult transition. Long-term selling requires patience and a tolerance for ambiguity. The sales person must be able to work effectively even without knowing whether she will succeed. Here is how you can help:

- **Screen job candidates carefully.**
  Hold long and probing interviews to determine whether the candidate has ever worked in a situation where outcomes were difficult to predict and involved a long waiting period. Psychological tests may help, if company policy permits their use and there is adequate business justification to use this kind of testing. This is a tricky area, so you may want to seek the advice of the human resource department or the company lawyer. Also, find out what is common in your industry before charging ahead with this kind of testing.

- **Coach, motivate, monitor.**
  Even the most confident sales person will sometimes be discouraged by long lead times. Keep her spirits up by focusing on the rewards if the sale is made. Ideally, you and your sales person will develop a strategy for each sales campaign, but it will be up to you to monitor it, to see that things are happening on schedule. Encourage the sales person to make contacts within the organizations being courted. Those contacts can be helpful in assessing her chances, as well as in advancing the sale.

FROM LONG-TERM TO SHORT-TERM SELLING

Again, screen carefully to try to determine the candidate's ability to adjust. But also watch for boredom. Experienced long-term salespeople are often overqualified for short-term selling jobs. Short-term selling may begin to seem dull and not challenging. Old pros may even begin to feel more like order takers than professionals. Help keep them motivated by handing them some challenges: To crack an account that has been firmly in a competitor's camp, for example, or to take on key account responsibilities.

Does Your Pay Plan Send the Right Message?

For best results, your compensation plan must support your company's goals. Does yours measure up? Check these critical areas to be sure:

- **The overall package.**
  Straight salary plans give you the most control over your people's activities; straight commission plans, the least. How do you achieve the right salary-commission mix? As a general guide, keep in mind that nonsales activities are nonrevenue producing. Therefore, the more nonsales activities you ask your salespeople to perform, the heavier you will want the salary component to be.

- **The basis for commissions and/or bonuses.**
  Incentives based on straight volume encourage salespeople to focus on those products or services that bring them the best return because they are either high-ticket or move easily. If your goal is to create a market for a new product, sell a certain mix of products or capture a certain size or type of customer, you will probably want to offer variable commissions, based on company priorities. Or, tie base pay to volume, while giving commissions and bonuses based on the attainment of specific goals. Just be certain that your plan is easy to understand and administer. Remember that incentives motivate best when your salespeople know precisely what they have to do to earn them and can track where they stand.

- **Quota setting.**
  Market potential can vary widely from territory to territory. Thus, for example, when you want to increase your overall gross revenues by 10 percent, it is futile and unfair to try to do it by simply increasing each sales person's quota by 10 percent. Instead, base your quota alterations on each territory's potential and the sales person's capabilities. For best results, also make sure that you measure market potential by product line, not simply overall.

Designing a Bonus Plan?

A strong bonus program supports motivation over the long term. Here are seven bases you can use to create bonus plans that will help motivate your salespeople.

1. Individual sales quota.

The bonus can be a flat dollar amount, a graduated amount corresponding to the percentage by which the representative surpasses the quota or an additional commission on sales over quota, which you pay out at the end of the bonus period.

2. Gross profit.

If this is your basis, give your salespeople a list of the gross profit margins of the products or services they sell.

3. Balanced selling.

This incentive is designed to encourage your people to sell a full range of products, services or lines. Be sure to clarify what constitutes the balance required to make bonus.

4. Selected products.

Here you want to focus on particular items or lines, usually your higher-profit products or services. Sales of other items do not qualify.

5. New business.

You can offer either a flat dollar amount based on opening a certain number of new accounts or an additional commission on new-account sales that exceed a specified base dollar amount. Yet another option: Pay the bonus on new business sold to established accounts–that is, on the sale of products, services or lines that the account has never before purchased.

6. Sales of accessories.

Make tie-in sales, sales of parts or add-on sales an incentive.

7. Sales related to promotions.

Use this bonus to help you move seasonal merchandise, holiday service specials and new or revamped products.

SURVEY PROFILES THE SO-CALLED AVERAGE SALES PERSON

It may well be argued that there is no such thing as a typical sales person or selling job. Each company, industry and territory presents specific challenges and opportunities. Still, it is always fascinating to find out who is in selling and how salespeople spend their time and are compensated. With that in mind, let us look at a compensation survey based on responses from more than 800 companies employing more than 90,000 salespeople. Here are some highlights:

Who Is Selling?

The average American sales professional is 36.8 years old and has been selling 7.4 years for the same company; 65 percent have a college degree. Of the respondents' field sales representatives, a greater percent are male.

How do They Spend Their Time?

Although sales activities and hours vary a good deal from industry to industry, the survey found that salespeople make an average of 3.3 sales calls per day and spend an average of 46.9 hours a week on the job. They spend 31 percent of their time in face-to-face selling (14.3 hours per week), 25 percent selling over the phone (11.6 hours), 18 percent waiting and traveling (8.5 hours), 15 percent on administrative tasks (7.2 hours) and 11 percent on service calls (5.3 hours).

How Many Calls to Close?

The average is 4, down significantly from an average of 5 in years past.

How Much do They Sell?

The salespeople covered by the survey bring in an average annual volume of $1.39 million apiece.

How Much do They Make?

On a company-by-company basis, the numbers were all over the lot, varying by company size, region, product or service, Industry and the type of buyer called on. Performance, of course, also makes a big difference. The better performers among intermediate reps earn 30 percent more than the average performer, while the best performers earn 58 percent more than the average.

Observation

Companies, both large and small, are spending more on training new hires as well as experienced salespeople, according to an industry survey. This is a strong indication that companies are willing to invest in the long-term success of their sales staffs.

Also, the percentage of companies that pay 100 percent of the sales person's expenses for a car, lodging, entertainment, telephone, product samples, local promotions, clerical help, photocopiers, PDA's, faxes, cell phones and laptops has risen across the board. About 86 percent of companies pay the full cost of their field sales reps' telephone and lodging expenses; 56 percent pony up the whole cost of a home fax machine; 41 percent, the full cost of a home copier; and 66 percent, the full cost for a laptop.

What Does a Sales Call Cost?

On average, each sales call costs $150, based on average compensation, benefits, field selling expenses, the number of calls needed to close and the dollar volume of the average sale.

Art and Science

As a sales manager, it is your responsibility to help your salespeople develop their skills and bring in the right customers and orders to meet your company's sales goals. This calls for a skillful blending of art and science on your part: Art in motivating your salespeople and science in managing the numbers and using proven sales techniques. To meet your company's profit goals, you will need to hone your skills in every key area of the sales process. As a sales manager, you have to stay on top of the numbers to ensure that your sales team's effort stays on course

Put these ideas and strategies into practice and you will go far toward optimizing your team is sales efforts and enabling them to perform at their highest levels. Some examples:

- **Recruiting applicants.**
  Based on your years of selling, you can wing a sales call if you have to. But do not try to wing interviews with job candidates, no matter how many you have conducted.

- **Coaching your sales team.**
  During a training session, wave that bag of gold back and forth. Remind your staff that the reward for taking back to the field what you are going to teach them will be more sales and more payback.

- **Motivating your salespeople.**
  If sales awards are passed out as casually as paychecks, they will lose their effectiveness as a key motivator of superior performance. The more pomp and circumstance you can provide the better.

- **Problem-solving via practical approaches.**
  If your sales reps are often hearing prospects say, I am not interested, chances are they are not qualifying effectively for need. Give your sales reps help in honing their qualifying skills.

2

Training & Coaching Your Sales Team

One of the most difficult tasks you face as a sales supervisor is being trainer, coach and mentor to your staff. Dealing with personality types ranging from the know-it-all veteran to the less-than-confident rookie is challenging, but it can also be very rewarding once you understand how to help your people maximize their talents. Use the techniques in this section to create a win-win situation for all: Helping you get better results from your sales force and showing your staff how they can utilize your expertise to their advantage.

TAKE THE CURSE OFF TRAINING SESSIONS

When salespeople balk at sales training sessions, it is usually because they resent being taken out of the field to be taught how to do what they are already doing. But even the most accomplished athletes, actors and musicians practice regularly–and sales training is a form of practice, too. To sell your salespeople on the training you offer, try these tactics:

- **Keep a narrow focus.**
  There are usually a few key problems that your salespeople find the most troubling. If the current list of complaints can be pared to just one, hold a training session dealing with that problem alone.

- **Avoid assigning blame.**
  You may be having problems with, for example, people writing orders

that do not meet the new minimum–quantity rule–despite instructions describing the rule in detail. But telling people: You dummies have been messing up and need to have things spelled out for you, will not bring you a lot of open minds. You are more likely to get their attention and cooperation with something like this: Those of you who are unclear about the minimum-order rule will find this session helpful.

- **Bring your people into the act.**

  Sometimes when you are joint-calling, a sales person will bring in a tough account, despite being thrown a curve ball. Once you have huddled afterward and agreed on what was done well (or might have been done better), tell him: We will be covering this situation at next month's meeting. It would be great if you could talk then about your success today.

- **Build in some smiles.**

  Some great laughs can result from a couple of seasoned salespeople playing, Can you top this? as they relate experiences relevant to the subject at hand. And there is nothing wrong with priming the pump just to get things started. Talk to a few of your more experienced salespeople before the session; they are bound to recall funny stories that are relevant, entertaining and instructive.

- **Make it optional for some people–sometimes.**

  Occasionally, you may want to make attendance for experienced salespeople optional. Then, when you are chatting with your salespeople, mention in a low-key way: Your input could be helpful to some people. If you would like to come, it might write a sale or two for you. That will get you more willing participation.

Recommendation

Survey people after each training session to find out if your message got through and if they thought the time was well spent. If there are any problems, you want to know about them right away.

Send Them Out on a High Note

Great training meeting, you think. The discussions were lively, people really got into the role-playing, there was a lot of sharing of good ideas. Now, if only they would take some of that back to the field, instead of forgetting it all the minute they walk out the door.

Your wishful thinking can become reality. Follow these pointers:

Open with a benefit sell. Tell your salespeople what advantages they will accrue from being there. "Before every such meeting, we poll the salespeople to learn what they are interested in hearing from us–in getting from us," says a developer of sales training programs. "Then we open the meeting by telling them what they are going to get out of it–which just happens to be exactly what they have told us they want. That is selling, is it not?"

Wave that bag of gold back and forth. Remind them that the reward for taking what you are going to teach them back to the field will be more sales–and more payback. The general sales manager for a marketer of agricultural chemicals says he reminds his salespeople how great it is going to be to make all that money, garner all those awards and feel so good about yourselves.

Add some flash to the flesh. Be careful about keeping talking heads on the platform too long. People's eyes will glaze over and your messages will not get through to them in the first place–meaning that they could not possibly put the techniques into practice.

It is usually more effective to break up long presentations with some show biz relief. Whether you satirize a tough customer by showing someone awaiting a sales person with a cocked pistol in hand or demonstrate a hard close by having a sales person enter and greet the customer similarly armed, punctuate your salient points with humor or drama. "I try to use every medium possible to break up the tedium," the sales trainer says.

Be an evangelist. Express your absolute belief in what you are teaching with all the golden-tongued oratory at your command. Get across your absolute certainty that it will work–you know because you have used it yourself. "We try to get them to open their minds to some new ways of attacking their problems," the sales trainer says. Then he offers them a money-back guarantee: "If it does not work for you, come back. We will talk about it and change it to fit your style and personality."

Reinforce both performance and purpose. "Salespeople are at their most effective when we get them into role-playing," the sales trainer says. "I reinforce their good examples at every opportunity." The agricultural chemicals sales manager tells his salespeople, "You are doing great. Now go out there and do a little greater because we have just shown you how." In the wrap-up, "I concentrate on the positives of what we have done–and send them out on a high note."

Observation

If there is one thing some salespeople hate as much as paperwork, it is training meetings. But if you sell them the idea ahead of time and keep selling it throughout the meeting, you will find that everyone will be rewarded.

GET THE MOST OUT OF A TOP TRAINING TECHNIQUE

You have read many articles telling you that role-play is one of the most effective ways to train your salespeople. But what does that really mean? Do you ask one of your salespeople to play himself and another to pretend to be a prospect and then let them wing it?

There is more to it than that and there actually are several kinds of role-play. Following are explanations of the most common varieties, with the pros and cons of each.

BEHAVIOR MODELING

Salespeople are asked to replicate, as closely as possible, a situation they have just seen. There usually are only two characters: the sales person and the prospect. The situation can be live, on video or on audiotape. An observer takes notes on the salespeople's behavior and leads a group critique afterward.

Pros

This is an excellent approach for new or inexperienced salespeople. Skills can easily be absorbed because the sales person does not have to think about the steps; she just needs to repeat them in the proper order.

Cons

Experienced salespeople will feel hemmed in. The technique can become boring with repetition and can be more of an exercise in memory than in skill building. It can be difficult (and expensive) to present models. Video or audio models may be generic rather than specific to your salespeople's situations.

TRUE ROLE-PLAYING

The sales person and the prospect are given separate information, not shared with the other party. Then the two are asked to play out the scene. An observer is given criteria by which to evaluate the role-play.

Pros

Different, even contradictory, information can be given to each party so as to approximate reality more closely. This challenges the sales person because no script is provided.

Cons

It requires a fair amount of expertise and work to construct the situations. In their efforts to create their next lines, participants may lose sight of the skills involved. Participants are more inclined to horse around; in particular, prospects may throw too many curves at salespeople. Thus, this approach requires close supervision by an instructor/trainer.

Team Role-Play

A customer situation is given to a group of salespeople and they are asked to develop and present a role-play based on it. Each team can create several roles in addition to the sales person and the prospect, for example, narrator, secretary/receptionist, competing salespeople and other staff in the customer's organization.

Pros

This can be a lot of a fun and a super morale builder. It allows for tremendous creativity and is an excellent choice for sales meetings or situations in which the final product will be viewed by many people.

Memo

Each type of role-play has a place. Begin by carefully considering what you want your salespeople to accomplish. Then choose the technique that best matches your specific training objectives.

Cons

It is a poor vehicle for teaching skills. Not everyone gets to play the role of sales person. Creativity and competition among teams can overwhelm the learning experience. A strong leader-guided discussion must follow to draw out and reinforce the learning points.

Help Salespeople Establish Credibility Fast

If you are a manager for, say, Bristol-Myers Squibb or AT&T, a buyer is not likely to respond with: Who? when one of your salespeople names the company she represents. But in most cases, the firm's name may be unfamiliar to potential customers. That leaves the prospect wondering: How do I know you will follow up on your promises? The sales person who neglects to answer that unspoken but crucial question risks losing sales.

Certainly you do not want your salespeople to focus on company over service or product. Still, it is worth reminding them that they should include company strengths in their presentations.

What can they focus on for your company? Here are some suggestions that can be adapted to showcase your firm's strengths:

- We were a one-product-line company when we began 10 years ago. But customers who appreciated our quality and service kept pushing us into one new line after another. Their satisfaction has continued, and they have made us a big small company now.

- A recent survey in an insurance industry journal rated us the most prompt payer in this part of the country, as well as the one that nitpicks customers' claims the least.

- Our current expansion will double our production facilities by year's end. From what I see of your operation, that will be important to your company.

- We have a phone group whose only task is to solve customer problems on the spot. If the phone service turns out to be insufficient, we guarantee that our service person will be on your premises within 24 hours.

- We make this product on a machine we designed and built ourselves. It will be a long time until the imitators catch up.

- Our unique engineering skills enable us to work with you to design and build any special equipment your situation requires.

- Success has led to our expansion, but it has not expanded our hat size. If you want to talk to someone in top management, you can count on getting a hearing—and you will not have to break through barricades.

- We are neither huge nor tiny. Because most of our customers fall into the same category, that makes for comfortable relationships.

- Our new owner is Bob Wilkes, who came here after leaving XYZ, where he was the marketing vice president. He has instilled in our company a strong customer orientation.

Observation

It is worth a training session to go over the details of the best points your company has going for it. With salespeople contributing their ideas too, you should be able to generate a pretty impressive list.

- We are actually a wholly owned subsidiary of Great American. That gives us the resources of a corporate giant, combined with the flexibility of a new, young enterprise.

- We have one person whose sole job is customer retention. He is constantly on the road checking on how customers like you think we are doing.

- Our vice president for customer service is part of our top management group.

We are not kidding when we talk about customer service—and she is not either.

Caution

Be sure to warn rookies not to let the company dominate the presentation and not to unload its virtues on customers in one big block. The goal is to let customers know the particular areas in which your company stands out while keeping the benefits of your product or service the focus of the presentation.

Do Not Let Cold Calls Give Your Salespeople Chills

The ideal way to get new business is by referral; it beats cold calling every time. But salespeople have to deal with the real, as well as the ideal and that means making cold calls. It is the rare sales person who truly enjoys cold calls. But you can make it easier for them by offering these pointers:

1. **Be street smart.**

   Cold calling does not mean heading off in six directions in a single day. That, of course, is a waste of time and very frustrating. Urge salespeople to use MapQuest as they comb the Yellow Pages, industry directories or other references so they can schedule as many appointments as possible within the same area. In major metropolitan areas, it may even be possible to identify several prospects in the same building. That way, salespeople spend less time on the road and more time in front of prospects.

2. **Warm the cold shoulder.**

   A sales person can turn the guard at a company's door into a facilitator by turning on the charm and not playing games about being a seller. One sales manager says, "My most effective salespeople walk away from that first cold call knowing the receptionist's name." Whatever clout the receptionist has with the boss is now working in the sales person's favor.

3. Qualify quickly.

One of salespeople's chief objections to cold calling is that they see it as a waste of time. But they have more control over that time than they may realize. Remind them that when a call is totally cold, they should qualify on the spot by probing–spending no more than 10 or 15 minutes doing so. If there appears to be some sales potential, the sales person can set up an appointment for a demonstration, an in-depth analysis of the prospect's situation or whatever is appropriate. If there is no potential–which, of course, is often the case–there has been little time lost.

4. Stick to the time bargain.

The sales person has not been budgeted into the prospect's day. Thus, he should say at the outset that the meeting will last a specified length of time. That becomes a contract. When the time is up, the sales person says: That is the 15 minutes you gave me. We can set up a new appointment–or we can continue now if you would prefer that. Whichever happens (and perhaps neither will), the sales person has credibility–and a good shot at a second call.

TELEMARKETING REGULATIONS

The Federal Trade Commission has several telemarketing regulations that apply specifically to business-to-business retail sales of nondurable office and cleaning supplies, such as toner, copier paper, cleaning products and so on. In other words, if you sell nondurable office and cleaning supplies directly to the users of those products–businesses, churches, sororities and so forth–you have to abide by the regulations. But if you sell such products only to resellers, you are exempt from them. If you sell to both types of customers, you must abide by the regs when selling to users. Here are the basics; you may:

- Call only between 8 a.m. and 9 p.m.

- State at the beginning of the call who you are and what you are selling.

- State that there is no purchase necessary to win if there is a prize promotion and also state the odds of winning the prize.

- Get written or taped authorization if money is to be taken from the customer's bank account.

- Disclose the total cost of your offer and any restrictions that apply before you ask for credit information.

- State that there is a no-refund policy, if applicable.

- Do not call people who have asked not to be called or registered on the Do Not Call Registry.

Why single out business-to-business sellers of nondurable office and cleaning supplies? Says an FTC spokesperson, "We have seen lots of abuses in those areas."

Good Record Keeping Can Cut Risks, Boost Sales

Careful record keeping can remove a lot of the guesswork–and thus the risk–from selling. Keeping records eliminates over-reliance on memory and can give salespeople a tangible picture of where they currently are with an account, where they have been and where they can reasonably expect to go. Your laptop should have up-to-date information, including the data from the sales reports generated by the company for internal use as well as summary sheets for client use.

But salespeople do not always understand the importance of such records and thus may not maintain them as well as they should. You can help by taking an occasional look at their records in several areas:

- **Where they are now.**
  What has each customer been buying? This is a key question, especially when you sell multiple lines. A specialty chemicals sales manager says his salespeople handle some 20 or 30 lines. We need to know which of those lines each account has been buying and even more, which ones they have not been buying.

- **Their best shot at each.**
  Your firm may have certain expertise that meets some customers' needs particularly well. But that expertise will pay off only if your people know how to exploit the advantage. A sales manager for a computer hardware and software company points out that, in her business, special needs are the order of the day and they seldom stay the same from one account to the next. So we must keep accurate records on which account has which problems. A sales person who does not remember what problems have been discussed will not know what he is going to talk about. The

simplest way to manage this process is to insist that the sales person keep a log or journal listing the issues (or special needs) and sending a confirmation of the sales meeting to the client, to you and to others in the organization on a need-to-know basis. Keep the copy list short and to only those who must and should have this information. (We all know people who send copies of e-mails to everyone in the organization!)

- **The stops along the way.**
  To increase sales, salespeople not only need a plan but also benchmarks against which to measure progress. "We want to get at least some and eventually all, of the business that now is going elsewhere," a branch manager says. That means salespeople need at least an approximate timetable for when they will sell account line A, followed by B and then C. Especially if the sales person is new, help them create this benchmark based on volume and potential volume from various customers. You and your team should be working off the same documents—everyone uses the same forms and the same operations to record activity and plan for the future. Do not let salespeople customize reporting and planning documents. It will double your work trying to read, digest and respond to them.

- **The roadblocks.**
  Competition is what keeps salespeople working, "We need to know who is getting what we are not getting and what their pricing is," says the chemical company sales manager, "and we need salespeople to tell us." That information can help management outline strategies for getting a bigger piece of the business. The marketing people can also be a huge help there, both in researching the various product lines but also competitor's prices, discounts, special offers and more.

- **Who said what, when.**
  "On large accounts," says the computer products sales manager, "there always are several people who want certain things delivered or capabilities included. We have to put in writing who said what and when. I do not want a sales person to say to a customer: Well, I think I told you we would have the new system installed by March 1st. Salespeople must know what everyone said, before and after the sale. Also, the technical people who do the follow-up on the salespeople's promises should put everything on record, too. Again, copies of e-mails and paperwork to the right people are absolutely a must."

- **The potential–both up and down.**

  Setting goals without knowing an account's potential is a futile exercise. A sales person's first goal is to keep an account of a customer. The next step is to estimate how much business is there and establish an ultimate goal– recognizing that it could change. Although failing to keep proper records inevitably will result in lost or overlooked business, and that is not the only reason to keep them. Evaluating the potential, by using records, also tells a sales person which accounts to drop.

HOW TO TELL IF SALESPEOPLE MAXIMIZE THEIR TERRITORIES

There are differences among territories: Some simply have a greater sales potential than others. There also are differences in account patterns. For example, over the years a senior sales person may have built up several large, profitable accounts that generate large revenues with very little attention. Meanwhile, a new sales person who is assigned the seemingly thankless task of opening up new business among what some companies call the Rest Of the World (ROW) may be on the other end of the scale.

The gross sales figures may obscure the fact that the younger sales person works much harder–and may be a better sales person–than the senior person who is coasting along on past glories. All this must be taken into account when evaluating a sales person's performance. You want to keep your eye on the big picture, but individual statistics may be more helpful as you work toward your managerial goals. These statistics are the numbers that report on individual sales performance by tracking activity volume.. They include new contacts, cold calls, qualified prospects, surveys, demos, proposals and closed sales.

Of course, these numbers are just raw data. By themselves, they tell little about the quality of the sales person's activity. Quality becomes somewhat more apparent when you use the raw data to deduce ratios. Ratios tell you how much of activity: A will produce how much of result B. The ratios most commonly tracked by sales managers are those that illustrate the ways prospects move through the prospecting funnel. For example:

- Number of new contacts leading to number of qualified prospects.

- Qualified prospects to presentations.

- Presentations to closes.

- Proposals to closes.
- And, finally, new contacts to closes.

The ratios can also alert you to problem areas. For example, if a sales person has a presentation-to-close ratio of 6-to-1–that is, it takes six presentations to close one sale–when the department average is 4-to-1, you can assume that the quality of this person's presentations leaves something to be desired. That ratio would not tell you the exact problem, but it will tell you where to begin looking.

Let Numbers be Your Ally

Sticking to the numbers when working with your salespeople has several key advantages:

Numbers focus discussion.
When you analyze the sales person's performance during a one-on-one meeting, the numbers will help both of you focus on where the discussion should be headed.

They eliminate much of the guesswork from managing the sales force.
Managers who do not monitor the statistical performance of their people at every step of the sales cycle find it difficult to explain why a sales person is failing to meet a quota.

Numbers are an early warning system.
If you know how many new contacts it takes on average to make a sale and you know the average value of a sale, then you know how many contacts a sales person must make in order to meet a quota. From there, it is an easy step to spotting problems before they become serious.

They help avoid confrontation and maintain the sales person's self-esteem. Numbers are neutral. They exist outside and apart from a sales person who may be having a performance problem. By focusing on the numbers–the facts–they create a neutral, analytical atmosphere in which to work with your salespeople toward improvement.

Memo

Being able to work with the numbers and making them work for you, requires two things: (1) a reliable reporting or tracking system and (2) a relationship of credibility and trust with your salespeople. Without the second item, any numbers you get will be suspect.

Self-Test: Do I Know Enough to Run My Territory Effectively?

Pretend that this test is an oral exam and the questions are coming at you rapid-fire. Take no more than 2 or 3 seconds to respond to each. Put a check mark in a box only if you are able to answer the question within that time limit. As such, your marks will not indicate a right or wrong answer—only the speed with which you reply.

1. How much does it cost per year to keep you in business? [ ]

2. What gross profits do your sales produce? [ ]

3. Do you have a 3-year sales target for your territory? If so, is it broken down by customer? [ ]

4. Are your recent sales gains real? Or do inflation and price increases account for most of them? [ ]

5. Have you expanded your market share in the past year for any product/service or line? At the expense of which competitors? [ ]

6. How much of your time is taken up by paperwork? [ ]

7. How much of your time goes to finding new business or gaining additional business from existing accounts? [ ]

8. What percentage of your work time is spent with key accounts? [ ]

9. How many sales leads do you average per month? Is that too many, or could you handle more? [ ]

10. Do you keep pace with customer problems and complaints rather than letting them pile up? [ ]

11. Do you keep a running tab on sales quotas and programs? [ ]

12. How many working hours a month do you spend in the office? [ ]

13. Is there a competitor about whom you have less than full information? [ ]

14. What key factors set you apart from the competition? [ ]

15. Do you feel that more training would help you do a better job? What kind of training? Have you spoken to anyone about getting this training? [ ]

16. Do you have accounts for which you know only a single buying influence? [ ]

17. Are you on solid professional terms with all your customers? Are there any exceptions? If so, do they include any key accounts? [ ]

18. Could you say in five to seven words why most of your customers do business with you? [ ]

19. Do you have a customer who accounts for one-third or more of your total sales volume? What do you plan to do if this customer drops you? [ ]

20. How many of your customers contribute no more than 2 percent to total sales volume? How much time do you spend with each of them? Do you call on them every month? [ ]

ANSWERS

It is important to be able to answer all the questions in the self-test, even if some apply only peripherally to your situation. Note that the questions fall into two groups. Numbers 1, 2, 6, 7, 8, 9, 12, 14, 18 and 20 call for hard, fast, specific, mostly numeric answers, replies not easy to think of under rapid-fire conditions. If you placed a check mark next to at least 5 of those 10 questions, you did well on that part of the quiz. Questions 3, 4, 5, 10, 11, 13, 15, 16, 17 and 19 were probably easier to answer with a check mark because so many call for yes or no answers. You did well if you checked at least 7.

Caution

A check mark means only that you were able to answer rapidly. It does not mean that your answers cannot be improved. For example, in response to question No. 12—the hours per month spent in the office—it is to your credit if you are aware of the situation. But that does not mean you are spending the optimal amount of time there. Some change or fine-tuning may be advisable.

TRAIN YOUR STAFF FOR TRADE SHOW DUTY

Selling at trade shows is different from field selling. Because trade shows represent a significant economic investment, it makes sense to train old hands as well as new recruits for this crucial selling environment. If you make it part of a pre-show strategy and review session for all those who will be staffing the booth, your more experienced people will not feel they are being forced to take training they do not need. Here are some suggestions to make these sessions productive.

Pinpoint Differences between Field and Trade Show Selling. Namely:

- The roles are reversed; the prospect calls on the sales person.

- The very fact that the prospect is at the show indicates an interest in buying.

- This is not a one-on-one situation. Many people, perhaps dozens, are streaming past the booth. Salespeople need to attract and work with the right people.

- The selling process is compressed. Sales calls seldom last more than 10 minutes.

Pointing out these crucial differences will alert your team to the need to shift gears and practice different strategies. Focus on the following areas:

- **Specify reasons and objectives**

  You are going to this show for a reason. Your salespeople should be very clear about that reason and committed to it. You may also want to tell them the budget for the show, to give them an added appreciation of their role. Review your goals for the team and for individual salespeople. How many qualified leads should each one bring in? To how many buyers should they present a new trade deal? Remember, inexperienced salespeople may feel that their goal has been set too high; that is usually because they do not fully appreciate the different dynamics of the trade show environment.

- **Training**

  A trade show sales call is not the same as a field call. Explain and role-play these steps:

- **Approach**

  Forget small talk. At a trade show it is business from the start. Salespeople should know which colors on name badges identify prospects (and which identify competitors!). If you want certain categories of prospects to be handled by certain salespeople, make sure everyone knows who is who. Work out an efficient way to route prospects to the correct sales rep. Once a sales person spots the right-colored tag, she should be ready with a selection of involvement questions: Are you familiar with the operation of this equipment? Do you use these services in your business?

- **Qualify**

  Is this prospect a qualified lead? A small lead card that fits in the palm of the hand is the most efficient way to record answers to a few key questions: name, company, address, line of business, decision maker or not the prospect's need. If possible, learn the time frame for making a decision and the available budget. But the key piece of information is need. Do you have a solution for this person's problems?

- **Present**

  At a trade show, a presentation that normally would take a half hour one-on-one must be condensed to a few minutes. That is why the sales rep must identify the prospect's need and then focus only on benefits that specifically relate to that need.

- **Close**

  At a trade show, closing means determining the next step (which is recorded on the lead card). It could be an immediate sale. More than likely, however, it will mean getting the prospect more information or setting up an appointment. You will need to find out how pressing his need is. Then sign the lead card and turn it in according to the instructions. Remind your people that qualified leads reduce cold calls.

Personal Behavior

Trade show booths are casual but professional places.

- **Adhere to the booth's schedule**

  The best way to ensure compliance is to have a reasonable schedule: 3 to 4 hours at a time is appropriate; never schedule a sales person for more than 6 hours straight. Fatigue dramatically reduces effectiveness.

- **Dress appropriately**

  Unless your booth's theme dictates otherwise, stick to business attire as it is usually defined in your industry. Comfortable shoes are a must.

- **Avoid the common breaches in courtesy**

  There should be no eating, drinking, smoking or gum chewing in the booth; these activities will project a poor image of your company. Also, no sitting–unless it is with a prospect in an area set aside for such meetings–and no chatting with colleagues. Both of these activities set up barriers for prospects.

WHO IS IN CHARGE HERE? ON A JOINT CALL, YOU ARE

Taking your firm's authority with you on a sales call–for example, an engineer or a computer expert–may be the key to closing the sale with an undecided prospect. But if your colleague, who is not the sales pro that you are, says the wrong thing or speaks at the wrong time, your strategy could backfire. How can you prevent such a disaster? First, remember that whatever the person's status or rank in her own department, it is your sales call on your prospect. Do not be shy about developing a call plan and giving her specific instructions on her role:

Offer a brief history of the account. Your colleague can contribute more effectively if she understands the context in which you are operating. Describe the company and your history with it.

"Recently, I took two marketing people to look at a couple of major retailers' stores before we called there," says a sales person for an optical products marketer. "I wanted them to get a feel for the account. We discussed their observations and then I gave them my opinion on where we stood. I give everybody–management, marketing, whomever–who walks into an account with me a pretty good idea of the significant factors. And I never forget to let the buyer know ahead of time who is coming with me on the sales call."

Prepare your colleague for the buyer you will call on. Your insights into the buyer's behavior affect your approach. Sharing this information is another way to help your colleague. After all, you cannot prepare a literal script for her, so the more guidance you can provide, the better her chances of offering appropriate support.

For example, is the buyer bright, chatty and likely to go off on tangents unless you steer him back? Be sure your colleague understands that–and also understands that you will do the steering.

Be absolutely clear about the objective and who calls the shots. This is where the greatest danger lies. A computer specialist might go on at length about the details of developing the program that makes your service unique–rather than focusing on the unique features themselves–and fail to see the customer's eyes glaze over. But by clarifying the tactics beforehand, you help ensure that the two of you will work in tandem.

"My engineer speaks only when his expertise is called for and only to the point," says a sales person for a marketer of testing instruments. "Other than that, he knows that I am in charge of the dialogue throughout the sales call."

The optical products sales person explains, "I prepare my colleagues by letting them know that this is not a hard sell and that we should not try to manipulate the prospect. The buyer and I are in business together to sell our product to the end-user. And we work together to do it. It is a low-pressure negotiation–a win-win situation. I am the negotiator. The visitor is the backup player."

Warn about the rules of the close. After you have asked for the order, you might decide that it is best to let silence reign. You do not want that silence to be shattered by an amateur—however well meaning. "Our people are trained to stay out of sales strategy," says the instruments sales person. "That keeps them sitting silently along with me."

WATCH WHAT YOU SAY ABOUT YOUR COMPETITORS

Suppose a prospect asks you to compare your product or service with a competitor's, feature by feature. Do you do it? Or suppose you have heard that another vendor is on the rocks financially. Do you pass the word to your customers? Even though you want to win business and keep your customers from getting burned, it is important to remember that all is not legally fair in love and war when the battle is on the sales front. To protect yourself and your company from legal action, you need to know about the law and how to respond to requests for product comparisons and industry gossip.

GROUNDS FOR ACTION

An unfair or untrue statement is grounds for action if it can be interpreted as damaging to a company's (or person's) business reputation. The person making the statement does not have to know that it is inaccurate and the plaintiff does not have to prove damages to win a settlement.

Lawyers say sales representatives who tell what they know would probably be on solid ground if they could cite an accepted outside source of their comments. But why get yourself into a tight situation when there are less risky ways to pass along what you know? Consider the following:

When you are asked for gossip or inside information: Instead of telling what you know, point the way for customers to find out for themselves. Say the customer brings up a concern about financial stability and you know your chief competitor has a problem in that area. You might handle it this way:

As you probably know, we have been in business for 50 years. We have had an A rating from Dun & Bradstreet every year for the past 3 decades our customers keep praising our continual product upgrades and quick response time when they need support. You mentioned Geff Corp. I believe I saw an article about them in a recent issue of…You might want to look it up.

Or, if you have heard about problems from other buyers, refer the customer to them:

I believe Victor Morales at ACG and Mary Jones at Kreuter have had some experience with Geff. You might want to call them.

Sometimes, of course, the customer is looking for information about his own competition because he knows you call on them, too. If he just hints for information, ignore the hints or refer him to published source material, if you know of any. If, however, he asks directly, be just as direct in saying:

I consider what you tell me confidential and would never pass it along to outsiders. I think you can understand that I have to do the same for all my customers.

The buyer may not like it, but consider the alternative. It is a sure bet that if you did spill the beans, in addition to losing the other customer and opening your company to possible legal action, at some point the buyer would start worrying that he could not trust you, putting your business with him in jeopardy, too.

When you are asked for point-by-point product comparisons: Give prospects the details on your own offering and emphasize your strengths in areas where you know your competition is weak. Support your claims with case histories, testimonials and technical studies. Then suggest that buyers ask the competition for similar information so that they can make their own comparisons. An even more effective approach is to emphasize

Recommendation

If your sales person feels he must make such comparisons, ask him to confer with you first and ensure the information he has is 100 percent accurate. Be just as sure the claims he makes for your own product are correct. Misrepresenting your offering can get you in as much legal hot water as misrepresenting a competitor—and can lose you customers as well. Merely claiming your product is better without specifically bad-mouthing the competition is considered puffing. Although it is not illegal, it is almost always ineffective.

your strengths and then refer prospects to satisfied customers who have experience with your product as well as the competition's.

Help Your Team Become Better Presenters

To be successful, your salespeople have to be able to present your total offering–what your firm offers in the way of customer support, delivery time, special terms and so on, as well as the features and benefits of your product or service. They also must be able to clarify for the customer the differences between your total offering and the competition's. Learning a full and thorough presentation will go a long way toward successful sales.

Two of the most effective ways to hone presentations are group training meetings with role-play exercises and one-on-one field coaching.

Effective Role-Play

To make the most of role-play exercises for honing presentations, work with small groups and plan to ease your least self-confident salespeople into their performances. The following tips may help:

- Let the super-confident go first. You undoubtedly have a few salespeople who consider themselves the cream of the crop. Let them play the seller's role in the first role-plays. They will demonstrate two points that should help the less confident: (1) Even the top people do not win every sale they go after, and (2) when they blow one, they are not blown away–other just go on to the next call.

- Assign the less confident to the customer's role at the outset. That gets them used to the spotlight without having to take any heat.

- Encourage those who are playing customers to draw their material from the toughest situations they have encountered in the field. Doing so will help elicit creative responses from those playing the sellers. That will mean more learning all around.

- Give those who are playing the sales person a special break. Generally, role-play sessions are played out only as far as the seller can go. If she fails to get the order, the role-play ends and the group critique begins. It can be useful, however, to let the seller stop the action when she is stuck and ask for suggestions from the audience–your other salespeople. That will increase participation and learning.

> - Insist on supportive critiques. Comments like–Never say that!–or–Handle it!–serve no useful purpose. They are more likely to destroy a sales person's confidence than to help her improve. Therefore, make it a rule that onlookers offer only positive suggestions, for example–Saying it this way might help you win more sales.
> - Chart the situations that give your people the most trouble. Also, track those on which there is disagreement about the most effective response. Use these as the basis for post-role-play discussion.

FIELD COACHING

Joint calls give you an opportunity to observe individual salespeople in action and help them develop. To work on presentation skills, observe the sales person and then rate him against a prepared checklist after each call: How well did he handle probing, demo materials, translating features to benefits and so on? Take 10 minutes between calls to analyze what went right or wrong. Start by asking the representative to rate his performance. Then focus the discussion on a single point. For example, if the person had difficulty making transitions into and out of the demo, explore that process and suggest possible solutions. If you think it would be helpful, let him observe you on the next call.

WORKING WITH ROOKIES

Working with the first-time sales person is usually equal parts of pain and pleasure. You enjoy the recruit's enthusiasm and eagerness to learn. You grit your teeth at the time required for initial support, field training and straightening out the almost inevitable goof-up or two. Let us take a look at ways to ease the transition from training to field.

Give the rookie a few, very specific goals to meet. His most important job is selling. For that reason, you want him to make as many calls as possible so that he can become comfortable with the presentation, get a feel for your markets and learn how to handle objections. Do not worry about balancing calls on A, B and C accounts right now. Just tell the rookie what percentage of his calls should be on established customers and what percentage on prospects. Also, give him two or three numerical measures he can use to assess how he is doing and be specific about what your firm considers an acceptable expense ratio (sales expenses to sales volume).

Stay in close touch. Ask for weekly reports and make time for one-on-one discussions. See to it that the rookie gets reports showing how he is doing vis-a-vis the measuring sticks you have given him. Let him know when he is doing well and reassure him when the numbers are not as good as they should be. Provide him with a list of backup people he can call when you are not available.

Field-coach as soon as it seems appropriate. During this initial coaching, let the representative watch you sell on, say, every other call. Critique only the critical points and do role-plays of handling major objections. Let the rest go for now.

Hiring Sales Veterans

You have just added an experienced sales person to your team. She has a great track record in another industry with a selling process that is virtually identical to your own. Given a little product and industry knowledge, she will be self-sufficient and you will be free to focus on other matters. Or will you?

However experienced newly hired sales veterans may be, it is unrealistic to expect them to produce at their old levels from day one. They will need coaching on your product, procedures and industry. Moreover, their sales methods may not work as well for them in the new situation.

It is your job to see to it that your new hire succeeds. Give her a thorough grounding in key product/service features, benefits and applications as well as company policies, procedures, goals and the accounts in her territory. Then let her make the rounds with a trusted veteran for a day or two. Once she is on her own, keep in close touch for the first week or two. Then schedule a series of joint calls to let your new hire observe you in at least one sales call and to give you a chance to spot practices your company discourages, such as high-pressure tactics.

Recommendation: If your new hire will be taking over the slot of a sales person who is being promoted or transferred, ease the transition for the hire, your accounts and yourself. Have the new person on board soon enough so that the outgoing sales person can introduce her to customers and show her the ropes. But do not make this an excuse to skimp on field coaching. She will still need your help to settle in.

Working with Mavericks

Working with mavericks usually brings out a love-hate response in managers. You love the results they achieve, but you hate the way they are constantly upsetting the apple cart–making caustic comments at district sales meetings, for example, or not showing up to receive a commendation from visiting brass because it would take valuable field time. Still, he is one of your best producers. What is a manager to do?

1. **Distinguish in your own mind between what is acceptable behavior and what has to change.**
   Activities that can get your company into legal trouble, anger upper management or demoralize other sales reps are unacceptable–period. Activities that are merely annoying can be overlooked so long as the maverick's sales record remains stellar.

2. **Let the maverick know where you draw the line.**
   Be explicit about which rules must be followed and what paperwork turned in. If the maverick has been undermining other sales representatives through his actions or comments, for example, call him on it. Cite specific examples of behavior that is out of line and how you expect it to change. Be direct. Mavericks can appreciate direct language.

3. **Stick to your terms.**
   While a maverick may threaten to quit, he is unlikely to throw his job away if you have been reasonable in your demands. Again, keep your list of musts as short as possible.

4. **Recognize the maverick's achievements.**
   Recognition is important to mavericks even if they act as though they do not care about it.

5. **Never ask a maverick to train others.**
   Mavericks simply are not capable of it. Even if they were, would you want a clone on your hands?

Coaching the Touchy and Argumentative

Coaching hyper-defensive sales representatives is extra challenging. They are so allergic to criticism that it can be difficult to help them correct faulty sales techniques or adopt new approaches. Still, it can be done. You just have to break through that defensiveness.

Overlooking Minor Faults

Focus on key issues and techniques and skip the minor faults you would mention when coaching less touchy reps.

- **Avoid unnecessary criticism.**
  Bear in mind that people who cannot admit they are wrong usually lack self-confidence and consider every criticism a personal attack. By focusing on key issues, you will not only minimize unpleasant conflicts but also spotlight areas that are most likely to affect the sales person's success. So when you do get the representative to try a new approach, it is likely to pay off for both of you.

- **Criticize the technique or situation, not the person.**
  No matter whom you are dealing with, this is the best approach. But with the thin-skinned, it is the only one that stands a chance. Negative comments with personal overtones simply put touchy people on the defensive. They get so busy justifying themselves (if only silently and to themselves) that they are not able to concentrate on your suggestions. Therefore, instead of saying: That response was weak or: That did not do the trick because…try something along the lines of, When buyers object, the response that is always worked best for me is…Or, be even more indirect and phrase your comments in terms of the buyer. These buyers never give up until somebody lays it right on the line to them.

- **Let the sales person respond.**
  Even oblique criticism is likely to produce a strong defense in this kind of sales rep. Let it flow. Ask questions to encourage the person to express himself. And do not get defensive yourself. You probably would not like a lot of what you will hear, but keep your cool. Make mental notes of key points to discuss later–after the person has finished letting off steam. Then be careful to separate fact from opinion and make concessions when and where they are justified.

- **Look for opportunities to praise.**
  Commend the representative every time he does something out of the ordinary, not just when you are coaching. Give him a sales call when call reports show an improvement in some specific area. Drop him a congratulatory note when he lands a key account. Thank him for useful suggestions. Even ask him to share his successful approach at your next sales meeting.

REACHING ARGUMENTATIVE TYPES

These are defensive people turned aggressive. Instead of withdrawing when confronted by criticism (the argumentative always see criticism as a form of confrontation), they fight it off. Instead of fighting back, try the following:

1. Persist calmly: You may have a point. Still…

2. Explain: Here is why I think it is worth another try…

3. Yield if you simply cannot get through, but put an edge in your voice: Well, if you would not even consider it…Often, that line will bring a response such as: All right. I will give it a shot if that is what you want.

Do not expect argumentative salespeople to yield graciously. Your goal here is simply to get them to try approaching the prospect in a way that you know will yield better results. Focus on those results rather than on the sales rep's irritating manner. As with purely defensive salespeople, make the focus of your remarks the customer, situation or objective, not the sales person.

Recommendation

Be on the lookout for relaxed moments when you can bring a specific problem out in the open and discuss it in a tension-free environment. Hyper-defensive people are most likely to lower their defenses when they do not feel under pressure.

FIELD-COACHING CHECKLIST

Field coaching is the tool of choice when it comes to developing sales skills. To make the most of your field visits, check yourself against the following list. The more of these practices you adopt, the more successful you are likely to be at your No. 1 task: developing field salespeople.

Preparing for the Field Trip

Let the rep know you are coming and how long you plan to stay. A week's notice is about right.

Review the rep's record; list probable coaching needs; select your prime focus for this trip.

Write down your main coaching objective; be specific.

Setting the Tone

Hold your initial meeting with the rep.

Share Your Objective

Go over the ground rules (your role as observer; how you will be introduced).

Encourage the Rep

Go over the day's (or next day's) scheduled calls and routing.

Suggest that the rep alert sensitive customers that you will be accompanying him on his next call. (Some buyers might resent an unannounced visit from a team.)

Before Each Call:

Review the rep's key objective

Ask for some background on the account. Example:

What products have we been selling them?

What share of their business are we getting?

Are there any problems?

Ask if there is anything special the rep wants you to watch for.

During Each Call

Observe and listen carefully. (Remain silent unless the customer asks you a direct question.)

Assess the rep in areas such as:

Establishing rapport.

Qualifying.

Assessing needs.

Listening to the customer.

Presenting the product/service.

Translating features to benefits.

Responding to doubts and objections.

Demonstrating the product.

Using proofs/testimonials/other sales aids.

Closing.

Product knowledge.

Competitor knowledge.

Overall attitude and helpfulness.

Note whether the representative:

Focuses on the call objective.

Avoids presenting any particular service, item or line.

Includes all pertinent information.

Is honest.

Maintains control of the call.

Does anything worthy of special commendation in your post-call conference.

Make a note of any new techniques/approaches the rep uses that are particularly effective and worth sharing with your other salespeople.

After Each Call

Ask how the rep thought the call went.

Comment on one major point.

Be specific.

Summarize (I think the main point to come out of this call is . . .).

Make notes for your wrap-up session.

At the End of the Day Visit

Review what the rep did well/poorly.

Get agreement on solutions to specific problems.

Coach or role-play as needed.

Get the rep's written commitment to specific changes/actions.

Follow-up

Send a thank-you memo.

Periodically inquire about how the new approach is working.

Periodically extend offers of help.

Encourage the rep to share her success stories.

Monitor progress versus the rep's signed commitment.

Recognize progress with a note or a phone call.

MAKE THE MOST OF CURBSIDE COACHING

The curbside conference is an integral part of field coaching. Between calls, you and the sales person briefly discuss the previous call and set goals for the next one. Here are some pointers for keeping your curbside coaching on track:

1. **Start with a question.**

   How do you think the call went? or How would you rate your performance? If the sales person is not wholly pleased with his performance, follow up with: What would you do differently next time? Use the reply as a jumping off point for adding your own insights.

2. **Focus your comments on a single point.**

   This is not the time to get involved in a lengthy critique or discussion of sales techniques. Instead, comment on one area, suggesting ways that the sales person can improve during the next call.

3. **Talk solutions, not problems.**

   I wonder what her reaction would have been if you had…Your solution lets the sales person discover the problem for himself–and that will make the lesson more valuable.

4. **Counsel in specifics.**

   Avoid giving vague advice. Instead, pinpoint particular improvements the sales person could make. For example, do not say: You could have converted more features to benefits, but rather, The built-in thermostat is an energy-saving benefit worth talking up.

5. **Keep the person in line.**

   Do not let the sales person sidestep an action you asked him to change or modify. For example, if you tell him that a certain promise he made puts the company on the spot, do not let a self-justifying response like: Well, I was not about to risk the sale; pass without comment. If you do, the sales person might take it as tacit approval–and that can mean trouble later.

6. **Summarize.**

   I think the main point to come out of this call is the way the customer kept trying to pull you into point-by-point comparisons with ACME's on-call service. That is a tough one to handle. Let us take some time tonight to role-play the situation. We can develop some responses that might work better.

GET A TRUE PICTURE OF SALESPEOPLE'S PERFORMANCE

"I know it is important to spend time with salespeople out in the field," says the district sales manager of a payroll services company. "But sometimes I wonder if I am getting a true picture of the way people perform. Maybe somebody who is usually pretty strong will just be having a bad day when I am there. Or somebody might schedule the kind of appointments that will make him look terrific."

You can get a more accurate reading of a sales person's performance and both benefit from the time you spend together. Consider these methods:

- **Give people appropriate notice of your visit.**

  Either too much or too little warning will skew your view. You may have some salespeople who are so eager to look good for the boss that they will take advantage of a long lead time to set up a series of calls on their friendliest accounts. Others, wanting you to know just how tough their territory is, may opt for all the prospects who are hardest to crack. Neither shows you the way the person functions day in and day out.

  By contrast, too little notice may upset those who need time to get used to the idea of the boss stopping by. I usually tell my people about a week ahead that, "I would like to make some joint sales calls with them," says the sales manager for a frozen foods distributor. "That seems to work best for me."

- **Let the sales person's schedule stand.**

  If you would like to see the sales person work with a particular kind of customer, say so at the time you announce your visit. Making such a change after you arrive would create two problems. First, it might endanger the sales person's relationship with the customer whose appointment must be canceled to accommodate your request. A sales manager for a machine tool marketer points out the second risk: "Even if it were practical, I would not ask a sales person to reschedule on the spur of the moment," he says. "I want to have a look at the way he schedules as much as the way he sells."

Recommendation

Make a point of reinforcing and praising good performance immediately after a sales call. Be as specific as possible, linking your praise to the sales person's personal development. For example, you might say: You handled that alternate-choice close beautifully. You should see your calls-to-sale ratio improve this month.

- **Be a silent partner.**

  Unless there is a special reason to intervene when you are on a joint call, avoid doing so. You are there to monitor. It is the sales person's customer. If you see something you do not like, you can ask about it later. If you intervene during the call, you give the customer the feeling that he is being used as a training ground. You also risk derailing the sales person's presentation and her relationship with the customer.

- **Try not to coach and run.**

  You might be tempted to squeeze visits to several salespeople into a few days. Spending less than 2 or 3 days with each one, however, erodes your ability to get an accurate view of how each one is doing—you may see just the good day or the bad day.

  "I spend about 3 days, if I possibly can," says the machine tool sales manager. "As much as the person may need coaching in selling situations, he also needs to see a manager just because he is alone in the field so much. The contact itself and the chance to unload personal problems, make it quality time for both of us."

- **Do not shorten the day as a reward.**

  Conscious of the sales person's positive response to the interaction, a manager might consider making it an even better occasion by quitting early. You can probably make a case for doing that, whether the person is selling particularly well—a celebration is in order—or having a tough time, in which case he could use a break. But the fact is, you would not then be seeing the sales person's real world.

  "There is a certain rhythm that a sales person establishes in a full day," says the frozen foods manager. "If you interrupt or break that rhythm, you are probably not seeing the person as he usually works. And that is why you are there."

Sometimes You Must Move to Center Stage

It is a joint sales call. You sit there biting your tongue, knowing that a few words from you could get things moving more smoothly. Yet you know that is not why you are there. Your role is strictly that of an observer. You must give the sales person free rein, allowing her to do the best possible job and work out any snags without your input. The time for you to make your suggestions for improvement is during the discussion that follows the call. That is gospel– and for good reason.

Yet there might be situations in which it is preferable for you to break the silence:

1. The customer pulls you in.

Many people feel the closer you get to the top, the more certain you are to get action. As a regional manager of a safety products company points out, "Sometimes a customer who sees me as a higher-up will shift the conversation to me. That can happen even when our guy already has called on him five or six times and there have been no problems. Somehow, though, the customer thinks he can get something more done with me."

Although a regional manager's intervention virtually guarantees a happy customer at the end of the call, he sometimes pays a price for it: From that time on, the buyer may continue to call on him to handle the most routine matters.

"I try to break that pattern by having the sales person get back with the response," the manager says, "but it does not always work." Because holding the account is primary, the manager then feels he has little choice but to service the account that has adopted him. If your sales person is upset by a similar turn of events, remind him that some customers feel they must deal with a higher-up. It is no reflection on the sales person or the job he is doing.

2. Your silence becomes a focus of attention.

The southern regional manager for an optical products marketer agrees that it is a better opportunity for a sales person to learn if I stay out of it altogether and critique when we finish the call. Sometimes, however, he gets a sense from the customer's body language–even just a look– that the person wants a contribution from him. Or, the visit starts to run a long time and I almost have to say something. Otherwise, I might give the impression of being a manager who does not command the subject matter. In either case, he makes his contribution and then passes the discussion back to the sales person. You have got to allow the sales person to sink or swim.

3. Special expertise is needed.

Some technical customers have requirements that salespeople are not equipped to deal with. "Even then, I would not take over unless the sales person specifically asks me to," says the safety products manager. "But I try to revert to being an observer as soon as I have given the technical information. I will say: "For additional information you can count on Mr. Jones here having all the answers. Then I drop out as smoothly and quietly as I can."

Recommendation

Whenever possible, hand the call back to the sales person. Otherwise, be prepared to assuage the sales person's ego after the call. However unavoidable your intervention, some salespeople may be a little shaken at having been upstaged. This is the case especially when you write the order. To end on an upbeat note, remind the sales person of her contributions, pointing out how she identified the prospect and its potential and made a good presentation. Be sure to acknowledge whatever a sales person did achieve during the call.

HELP HONE PRE-CALL SKILLS DURING FIELD VISITS

The objective when preparing for a sales call is to get ready to make the most effective presentation possible. That means having a thorough knowledge of the product or service, as well as a clear picture of the customer's needs.

Clearly, salespeople have a lot of ground to cover in preparing for a sales call. Your field coaching visits are an excellent opportunity for you to help them strengthen their call-preparation skills. Meet with the sales person beforehand. Allow at least 1 hour of conference time before the first sales call.

- **Briefly discuss the calls the person has scheduled for the day.**

- **Get a rundown on routing and the travel time between calls.**
  You may want to question the person's routing if it does not appear to be as efficient as possible.

- **Give the sales person the leeway to introduce you to each customer.**
  Make sure he uses the manner he chooses as manager, sales supervisor or whatever. (The sales person should have alerted each customer to the joint call as soon as he knew about your visit.)

- **Emphasize that your role during all calls is that of observer.**
  The exception is the call or calls during which you have agreed in

advance to reverse roles. Advise the sales person that, as an observer, you will respond to a customer only if questioned directly—and that even then, you will do your best to bounce the question back to the sales person.

- **Discuss the upcoming call.**

  The key question for you to ask is: What is your objective on this call? Inquire into the strategy for achieving the objective and ask for some background on the account:

  - What services/products have we been selling to them?

  - What share of their business are we getting now?

  - Are you dealing with the top buying influence?

  - Is this account solid or shaky?

  - Are there any specific problems with the account?

  - How might we increase our sales here?

- **Ask the sales person what he would like you to assess.**

  Some salespeople are aware of personal shortcomings and would welcome a targeted critique. A useful—and non-threatening—question to ask: As far as your selling goes, is there anything special you would like me to watch for and comment on?

- **Do not dominate the pre-call conversation.**

  That can build pressure and it limits your opportunities to get valuable input from the sales person. Your objective during the pre-call is to see how the person prepares and to set a tone that will help the representative go into the call in top form.

- **Be pro-company in all your comments about your firm.**

  For example, if the sales person says: Acme's lower price prevents me from getting more of XYZ's business, do not validate the remark by replying: I know what you mean. Instead, role-play the point with the sales person. Coach him on overcoming the price objection by selling value.

- **Use a motivational approach.**

  Bear in mind that the person is about to go into action in front of the boss as well as the customer. Use positive suggestions to build the sales person up, rather than tearing him down with negative comments.

- **Be supportive.**
  Point out that the sales call is not a test.

- **Avoid the parent-to-child approach.**
  Do not say things like: You should do…You ought to try…Let the sales person decide what will be done in front of the customer.

- **Use team language.**
  Say: we, not I, whenever possible. Reinforce the feeling that you both are on the same side.

ARE YOUR REPS PHYSICALLY PREPARED FOR THE CALL?

Field coaching offers an ideal opportunity to help your people sharpen their preparation skills. Your objective is to make sure that the representative has done her homework, set a specific goal for the call and work up a plan to achieve it. But you also must rate the sales person's appearance and readiness and work with her on setting goals for improvement, should any be needed. You may want to use or adapt the physical preparation checklist on the next page to rate your sales representatives' appearance and readiness.

Preparation Checklist

Clothes clean, pressed and in good condition.	
Shoes shined.	
Car clean inside and out.	
Trunk organized.	
Road maps, Internet directions, GPS set.	
Business cards on hand and in good condition.	
Sales history of the account, if any.	
Briefcase clean, in good condition and organized.	
Orders and status reports prepared and on hand.	
Literature up-to-date and in good condition.	
Comparison sheet with competitors' products.	
Samples, visuals, cutaways, demo pieces complete, clean and accounted for.	
Testimonials up-to-date and appropriate for planned calls.	
Manuals, catalogs up-to-date and in good condition.	
Price lists up-to-date, clean and easy to read (not poor-quality photocopies).	
Order forms clean and ready to use.	
Laptop charged up and power adapter cord on hand.	
Accessories on hand (phone, Blackberry, adapter).	
Note pads and pens at hand.	
Printed materials and equipment for demos checked and in place.	
PowerPoint presentations, printed and on the laptop.	
Live demonstrations on the laptop.	
Appointments and reservations confirmed.	
Credit cards and cash as needed.	

Motivating Your Salespeople to Continued Success

3

It is not enough today for you simply to be good at sales and managing the sales process. You must also be able to inspire your sales team during difficult times. Boosting the morale of your salespeople is as important as ensuring they have the right tools and training to exceed their sales goals. In this section we will show you how your sales force can learn to weather the rough periods without losing perspective and produce more positive results even during tough situations.

GET MAXIMUM BENEFITS VIA INCENTIVE AWARDS

Incentive awards can be a major motivational tool for your salespeople. But as with all positive reinforcement, incentive awards must adhere to basic motivational principles:

- **They must be specific.**
  Singling out the top producer is not enough. Also-rans must understand what skills and behaviors produced the final numbers.

- **They must be meaningful.**
  The awards must recognize an achievement that required genuine effort and was, in some way, above the norm. Otherwise, they insult the capability of the recipient and downgrade the value of the award in everyone's eyes.

- **They must be timely.**
  If it is a Sales Person of the Quarter award, present it as soon as possible after the numbers hit your desk. The longer you wait, the more the stresses and challenges of the quarter will recede in your staff's memories.

- **They must be regular.**
  To achieve their full potential, awards should be an accepted, anticipated part of field routine. The effect will be cumulative with each successive award period generating more team spirit.

PRESENTATION COUNTS, TOO

Reinforcement will not work if it is delivered offhandedly. Nor will it have its intended impact if it is perceived as insincere or forced. The most effective way to present awards, of course, is at public ceremonies, usually your sales meetings. Present top awards at the annual sales conference. If the entire sales force and many support people are present, the awards can serve as motivators for everyone, not just the honorees.

Here is how to get the maximum motivational punch from those ceremonies:

- **Spell out what the awards are for.**
  Money is the way salespeople keep score and everyone wants to know the score. Do not confine yourself to saying: Susan booked $800,000 in sales this quarter. Point out that was 125 percent of her quota, or that it was her highest quarter ever, or that it was just $10,000 shy of the all-time quarterly record. Your goal is to encourage all your people to quantify their goals and analyze their performance against historical benchmarks.

- **Link sales success to selling skills.**
  Make it clear that the winner's superior performance was not just a matter of luck. Point out specific techniques or skills the person used to achieve her numbers. This will remind both the winner and the listeners that you, the manager, value proper technique as well as the bottom line.

- **Invite the winners to say a few words.**
  There is much to be gained by having your top performers share their experiences. The achiever will be able to tell a war story and enjoy the

spotlight and the benefits of sound sales strategy will be reinforced for the rest of the sales force. Alert winners in advance that they will be asked to speak briefly at the ceremony.

- **Close with a look ahead.**
  Wrap up the awards ceremony with a few words on the challenges that lie ahead and an exhortation to the troops to put forth their best effort.

How to Move Old Pros Off Their Plateaus

Chances are, you have one or two old pros on your sales team–salespeople who have been with your company 5, 10 or more years, who are not interested in moving into management but bring in steady business. Trouble is, steady business is not enough for most companies these days. They expect growth and it is your job to produce it. To move old pros of any age off their plateaus, try these tactics:

Enrich the Job

Give the pro a larger or more lucrative territory or a broader base of active accounts (for example, by turning over some company accounts, if you have them). Ask the person to take on a specialized assignment that requires selling across several territories. Increase the person's non-selling responsibilities, for example, by asking her to help train new hires. A training assignment can be particularly effective here: The pro will give herself a refresher course in sales techniques as she works with the new hire and she will also want to demonstrate her selling expertise.

Give Them More Discretion In Working with Customers

Your people probably have to consult with you on matters of negotiating price, customizing large orders, holding price increases in abeyance for 2 to 3 days and so on. Your veterans have been with you long enough that they can probably predict your response. So why not give them the discretion to call these shots themselves? Then back up their new authority with a new title, such as Senior Sales Person or Master Sales Person. That will increase their status in the eyes of their customers as well.

Observation

If sales awards are passed out as casually as paychecks, they will lose their effectiveness as a key motivator of superior performance. The more pomp and circumstance you can provide, the better.

Publicly Recognize their Expertise and Contributions

Ask your experienced people (not just your stars) to speak at sales meetings. See to it that their stories appear in the company newsletter. Recognize their years of service and special contributions with plaques or certificates presented at sales meetings with appropriate fanfare. Public recognition piques motivation and gives all your people an incentive to keep stretching.

Memo

If you assign additional non-selling duties, such as training, adjust the sales person's compensation to reflect them so that your enrichment effort does not sap motivation.

WATCH OUT FOR KILLER CRITICISM

"The job that most managers–sales managers included–bomb is criticizing subordinates." So says Hendrie Weisinger, author of *The Critical Edge*, a book on criticism techniques. "Criticism is the most important managerial skill," he says, "yet only two in 10 use it effectively."

Weisinger's two key rules: (1) Do not attack and (2) criticize performance, not the person. Reason: The meat hook method never boosts performance and may actually diminish it by injuring a person's self-esteem. Other guidelines:

- **Practice empathy**
  Try to imagine how the person on the receiving end feels about
  the criticism.

- **Criticize positively**
  Convince the individual that you know he can improve.

- **Be a good listener**
  The best criticism is a dialogue, not a monologue.

- **Criticize privately**
  A public dressing-down can injure the morale of the entire sales team.

- **Follow up**
  Set a deadline for improvement and check up on progress.

FIND THE CAUSE OF A SLUMP BLAMELESSLY

Observation

If you find that you spend too much time criticizing salespeople, it may be a sign that you are not communicating your goals effectively.

Joint sales calls usually are a good way to discover why one of your salespeople is in a slump. But if the sales person insists she is not at fault, the joint call may only confuse matters. The sales person may resent the fact that you think she needs to change—when as far as she is concerned, the problem is the economy, that new competitive product or even a problem with your own line or customer-support package. When that is the case, you will not get an accurate picture of the person's performance simply by making joint calls. Instead, you will have to find a way to get the person to tell you. Here are some suggestions:

Keep the Playing Field Level

You are the boss and your bringing up the subject underlines who is in charge. Nevertheless, maintain a collegial attitude in both your voice and manner. You want to generate as little heat as possible to improve the chances of shedding some light on the problem.

Keep the Setting Neutral

Avoid your office or, if you are on the road, your hotel room. Holding your discussion in a restaurant or even in the sales person's home or hotel room will reduce the pressure. Your objective is to probe gently, not to grill. You want to play counselor, not cop.

Eliminate Time Pressure

Rather than saying, Let us take an hour to see if we can find out where our perceptions differ. Leave out the take an hour to and finish with even if we have to cancel this afternoon's calls. The reason: The sales person's thoughts may be in a jumble: Is anything really wrong? Do I know what it is? Should I tell him? I do not know what it is, or I would have fixed it by now. How can I come up with the answer in an hour? All those uncertainties create more pressure. Giving the person an hour to confess or come up with a solution may further tighten her emotional state.

Start the Agenda in a Low-Key Manner

Come at it as a customer problem, rather than the sales person's problem: I see that Circuit Board has reduced its order quite a bit and Robotics is dropping off some, too. What are they doing anyway? That states things as a customer problem.

Whatever response the sales person gives you will be similarly couched: They have a new buyer or, all of a sudden, they are getting uptight about price. OK, so the sales person sounds like a spectator rather than a participant—but at least now you have something to sink your teeth into.

Conceal Your Fangs

You may be thinking: Oh, come on, so what else is new? But do not say it. Uptight people need to be treated gently. Instead, say: So, I guess that is why you have been calling on them less. Your apparent acceptance of her inactivity may relax the person enough for you to follow with: Tell me a little about the new buyer or when did he begin complaining about price?

Observation

The sales person may never admit there has been a slump, even after she recovers. The truth is, it does not matter. As long as the person begins to recover her usual style and results, you have achieved your goal. That is what counts.

Keep the Discussion Going

If the person relates what she has been doing, or not doing, you can suggest: Did you ever think of . . .? If you manage to keep it very cool, one of two things is likely to happen. The person will commit casually to trying your suggestions. Or, if you can sell some immediate joint calling, she may even try out a suggestion right away, giving the two of you an opportunity to assess the results. Whether the suggestion works or not–and chances are it will be at least partially successful–discussing the results will give you further opportunity to probe and correct the basic problem.

Help Your People Get More Proof Letters

Showing a proof letter–a testimonial from a satisfied customer–to an almost-decided prospect can be highly effective. Yet salespeople do not use this tactic as often as they might. The reason: They find it awkward to request such letters and fear that even the most satisfied customer would not want to put it in writing.

The following guidelines from you can help your salespeople get around that hang-up. If they focus on the instances in which there is a solid basis for making the request, salespeople thus have a better chance for a positive response.

- **Advise against requesting blanket endorsements.**
  Your computer services may have reduced a customer's payroll costs, resulted in fewer errors in his salespeople's commission payments and revolutionized his inventory control. However, unless the buyer is the sales person's brother, he simply is not going to write all that down. But if the sales person asks him to write an acknowledgment of the great

assist he got in just one of those areas, the sales person has an excellent chance to succeed. The request should involve proof of the results that have the widest application in your market.

- **Show how to seize opportunities.**
  A customer with whom a sales person has a run-of-the-mill relationship is not a promising target for a proof-letter request. But this customer may occasionally express particular satisfaction: I must say, the way you guys came through on that rush delivery impressed me. I never really thought you would, you know. Pounce! Respond: Mr. Jones, if you would put that in a letter to me, I would be one happy sales person. That requires making just one close, but the sales person's chances of getting what he asks for are good.

- **Use occasional field surveys.**
  A couple times a year, ask your salespeople to carry along a short questionnaire that deals with the half dozen most important sources of customer satisfaction or dissatisfaction. You will learn a lot about the areas in which you need to improve, as well as those in which it would pay to expand on what you are already doing well. Whenever a customer's responses all are positive, it is reasonable for the sales person to ask for permission to show the questionnaire to prospects. If the answer is yes, the sales person can then ask the customer to sign the form itself. And there it is–an instant proof letter.

- **Remind salespeople of the need for stroking.**
  When a prospective account is sitting on the fence, a small nudge will sometimes make the difference. If that nudge could be supplied by a proof letter from a particular customer, your sales person can be straightforward about saying so: I have a shot at landing United this week. A letter from you that says I do a good job could bring it in for me. You are an industry leader, after all. Would you be willing to write a note for me? Again, this is a one-close effort   the odds are in the sales person's favor.

Observation

These guidelines will help your salespeople zero in on targets of opportunity. Taking that rifle-shot approach will result in fewer requests and more positive responses.

Help Salespeople Move the Customers on Hold

When economic times are uncertain, you will find some customers on hold, waiting for a prognostication they can believe or for a strong gust of economic wind itself to convince them to act. But it is not likely to have arrived by the time your salespeople call. So your salespeople hear: Well, the way things look, we think we would better wait a bit. There are ways to help your salespeople move those waiting customers into action.

Head Set May Need Adjustment

You can give your salespeople a series of effective responses, run a sales meeting to strengthen them, even do some joint calling to demonstrate their efficacy. But it all will be to no avail if your people buy the customer's excuse– if they themselves are feeling uncertain. "So before you work on the most effective responses, work on their heads." Says a metalworking products sales manager, "I have been trying to condition our salespeople by telling them, do not worry about the economy; worry about what you personally can impact. Then do the best job you can to influence your customers."

Customers Cannot Sell from an Empty Wagon

A business that is unprepared to fill orders as they come in has a serious marketing problem: It surely will lose customers. The metalworking sales manager reminds his salespeople to convey to customers that they should not worry about the macroeconomy. In any economy, the opportunities are out there, he emphasizes. When a company finds them and exploits them, it has to be able to deliver the goods. That usually begins with buying something from your sales person.

Emergency Orders May be Hard to Fill

Some customers count on being able to get short-notice delivery of materials or products they will need when they get orders they are not currently counting on. The sales manager urges his salespeople to point out that when that kind of situation develops, it usually is widespread. Lead times quickly grow longer and many buyers end up waiting unhappily for back orders. Therefore, now is still the best time to buy.

Decisions Must Make Good Business Sense

A regional manager for a marketer of electronic security systems says that his people often hear something like this from customers: We are still talking about more downsizing here. This certainly is not the time for me to buy anything I do not have to. The response he finds most effective: Well, with fewer people around, the danger of company property disappearing is that much greater. Installing a security system makes good business sense.

Memo

The message to both salespeople and customers is that you cannot be sure of the future, so it is important to take care of current business now.

The Wait for Falling Prices May be a Long One.

When customers give as the reason for their hesitation the possibility that prices may fall, they hardly believe it themselves. That rarely happens in the business-to-business marketplace. When the economy shows signs of strength in various geographic areas, the only concern about prices in some industries is not whether they are going up, but how far they will climb.

HOW TO MAXIMIZE MOTIVATION

No matter how enthusiastic salespeople and their managers may be about their profession, there is one aspect that they all dislike: constant rejection. Those who remain in the profession have learned to handle rejection. People who cannot cope with rejection either do not choose or do not remain in sales.

Memo

You probably need even more self-motivation than your salespeople to serve as their coach, mentor, psychologist and mediator. While handling your operational responsibilities and interacting with your peers and managers, you have to be concerned about your salespeople's self-motivation as well as your own. Obviously, self-motivation is something that one cultivates within oneself; you cannot create it for others. Still, you can encourage your salespeople to work on their self-development.

At a sales meeting or training session, schedule a time for salespeople to read this section and take the quizzes. Do not follow up with a discussion—these are intensely personal self-analyses that people should think about individually. Instead, urge your people to do their own follow-up, reaching within themselves to determine what the quizzes reveal about areas they should explore and steps they can take to move in the right direction. Encourage them to get specific about the latter—good intentions are not enough.

Use that same session to read and think through this section yourself. The material will give you greater insight into salespeople's concerns—concerns that you once might have had but that you sometimes lose sight of after becoming a manager. Even though your day-to-day responsibilities have changed, the motivational principles are the same for everyone. As such, you also can benefit from an occasional motivational boost.

What enables successful sales professionals to keep going despite the kind of rejection that could devastate others? Their high level of self-motivation. Although having a product or service they believe in and finely honed sales skills are necessary, they are not enough. What a sales person needs, above all, is an extraordinary level of confidence and the ability to maintain that level throughout a career.

How do you do that? How can you keep yourself charged up, day after day, if prospects keep turning you down? If you have ever been in a sales slump who has not? You may sometimes wonder if you have the drive to make it in sales. You do. The motivating force that you need exists within you, but it must be cultivated. In this section we will explore how to go about it.

SELF-TEST NO. 1: HOW DO YOU FEEL ABOUT YOURSELF?

Answer each statement below and keep in mind that this is a guide, not a test. Then check your answers against the Preferred Answers on page 84. For each point of disagreement, ask yourself: Can I do something about that point? Do I want to?

	True	False
1. I weigh my accomplishments against my expectations.	[ ]	[ ]
2. I am easily upset.	[ ]	[ ]
3. My job is routine.	[ ]	[ ]
4. I tend to push problems aside.	[ ]	[ ]
5. I enjoy being friendly.	[ ]	[ ]
6. I shy away from the unfamiliar.	[ ]	[ ]
7. I can laugh at myself.	[ ]	[ ]
8. Bad news puts me in a bad mood.	[ ]	[ ]
9. Some people intimidate me.	[ ]	[ ]
10. Some people take up too much of my time.	[ ]	[ ]
11. I often think about better ways to do things.	[ ]	[ ]
12. I hide my feelings from others.	[ ]	[ ]
13. I am not easily or often fooled.	[ ]	[ ]
14. I make changes when I have to.	[ ]	[ ]
15. I can be nasty when I have to.	[ ]	[ ]
16. I think other people are as good as I am.	[ ]	[ ]
17. I worry about failing.	[ ]	[ ]

DEVELOPING YOUR SELF-IMAGE

Self-image is the way you feel about yourself. If your self-image is not healthy, it is unlikely that you can increase your motivation. If you have ever experienced yo-yo motivation—up one day, down the next—chances are, the image you have of yourself is not very positive.

Your feelings about yourself can be changed. Think about some of the things people do to grow and thus improve the way they feel about themselves:

- They read books they would not have picked up in the past.

- They try to perfect a skill.
- They go back to school.
- They go on diets.
- They exercise.
- Some even change jobs.

The list of possibilities is endless; the decision is yours to make.

When you are sold on yourself and value your responsibilities, you know instinctively that it is in your self-interest to push yourself when necessary. Your self-image supports your professionalism and pride. It reminds you of the standards you have set for yourself, standards to which people you want to please–family, friends, customers, colleagues–have become accustomed.

When you are at odds with yourself or ill at ease with your responsibilities, your everyday concern is to make it through, cover up and live to do battle another day. When that is the situation, your self-image is the enemy, although you may not be aware of it.

SHAPING YOUR ATTITUDE

Read any book on the selling profession and you will find extensive discussions of attitude. Check any list of what it takes to succeed as a sales person or manager and you will find the word attitude again and again. Ask any manager what she looks for in a sales person and she will talk about the importance of the right attitude. Why so much emphasis on it? Because in selling, attitude is your motivational position. It is what self-starts you every morning, what pushes you into accomplishments that some salespeople rarely experience. Without a strong, positive attitude, you are not likely to excel in the sales profession.

Attitudes are not set in concrete; they must be monitored and maintained. You can gradually lose a positive attitude if you become complacent, or you can reshape a negative attitude if you work hard. If you are looking for a greater motivational payoff from your attitude, here are some things you can try:

- **Practice the art of positive thinking.**
  To begin, get rid of the idea that work and fun are mutually exclusive. Your attitude toward work can be serious without being humorless. Remember

that a sense of humor has a place in a business relationship and will actually strengthen it.

- **Do not be a complainer, even to yourself.**
  Do not be a person who has a negative attitude and complains about losing a sale and assigns blame. A person with a positive attitude looks toward getting something other than sorrow out of the situation. Only a fool would be happy about a lost sale and only a fool would fail to learn something from it. That is the beauty of attitude–a good one today helps you tomorrow.

- **Work with a vision, not just a goal.**
  Necessary as goals are, they can be dry. Visions are glorious. Suppose you hunger for more respect from certain people (and if you do, you are not alone). You would feel sensational–extremely proud of yourself–if you got it. The thing to do, then, is to begin every day with a single question: What can I do today to come closer to that vision? You may find that what once were chores are now just plain work and not that bad. This can occur when tasks become stepping stones to realizing your vision.

- **Use common sense to counter negative attitudes.**
  A single negative attitude can turn you into a negative person. That is death in sales. For example, suppose you do not think there is a need for what you do–a depressing concept! To counter it, think: How many people are using what I sell them to their advantage? How many customers are happy with, or make money because of, what I sell them? In this way, you can feel good about your contributions to the lives of others. Never believe that you have reached the top. When you believe that you are doing about as well as you can and selling as much as you can, you are already on the way down. Your attitude responds in kind and there goes your motivation.

SELF-TEST NO. 2: ARE YOU LIKELY TO EXCEL?

Check **Yes** or **No** for each statement, then turn to page 86 to see how your attitudes stack up against the preferred answers.

	Yes	No
1. A lot of money can be made in sales.	[ ]	[ ]
2. I prefer a straight salary so I can better plan my life.	[ ]	[ ]
3. If I were a smoother talker, I could earn more money.	[ ]	[ ]
4. I like being on my own.	[ ]	[ ]
5. I do not think I get much respect being a sales person.	[ ]	[ ]
6. I wish I had a nicer clientele to call on.	[ ]	[ ]
7. I learn more about people all the time.	[ ]	[ ]
8. I am tired of people pleading poverty.	[ ]	[ ]
9. I lose more sales because of price than any other factor.	[ ]	[ ]
10. Most of the sales leads I get are worthless.	[ ]	[ ]
11. I know there is a need for what I do.	[ ]	[ ]
12. I know my business from A to Z.	[ ]	[ ]

SETTING AND MEETING GOALS

How can I psych myself up every day? How can I get motivated? One way not to do it is to go on a crash-psyching binge, which, like a crash diet, has you flying high for a week or two and then, like any bad experiment, burns out. When it comes to motivation, it is not burnout you are after, but an iron will.

One way to power up and prolong it is through target setting. Targets are not chores; they are short-term goals–1 day, 1 week, 1 month, maximum. They pay off now, not 5 years from now, so they fuel your motivation. Moreover, target setting is a motivational system that you control. It is up to you to set levels that are high enough to enjoy stretching for, but not so high that you blow up the system.

SET ACTIVITY TARGETS

A target is something you can see—it has a bull's-eye. With concentration, you can hit it: I am going to make 12 cold calls a week is a target. In setting targets, forget money, closing sales, hope—forget anything that is not in your power to achieve alone. Activity targets deal in numbers that you can count on because you control them. Targets spur you to increase an activity and because you do more of it, you are bound to get better at it. In fact, the more games you play, the more you will win.

Look at it this way: Suppose you average one sale every five calls and are in the habit of making five calls a day, or 25 a week. If you increase your activity to six calls a day, or 30 a week, you should make an extra sale every week even if your average remains the same.

Here are some targets to consider:

[ ] Referrals (from existing accounts)

[ ] Prospecting calls (cold calls)

[ ] Telephoning (appointments/sales)

[ ] Mail-outs (sales letters, sales reminders, brochures)

[ ] Selling hours (actual selling time spent with prospects
   and customers)

[ ] Key accounts (time spent with big-potential buyers)

[ ] Accessories, service contracts, collections (time spent on areas that
   need more work)

[ ] Lost accounts (time spent with ex-customers)

[ ] Future file (time spent with prospects who were never sold)

[ ] Service-call conversions (time spent on selling during necessary
   service calls)

[ ] Unpleasant tasks (see below)

AN EXCEPTION TO THE RULE

An unpleasant task is a thorn in your side, demotivator, in most cases. That makes it an exception to the rule that you will enjoy stretching yourself to reach an activity target. But consider this: Unpleasant tasks will give you more satisfaction, after the fact, than any other targets.

Unpleasant tasks are those that you dislike or fear. They tend to lead you right down the path of procrastination. The nasty customer you hate to call on, but have to, can gnaw at you and affect your attitude all week. Then there is that major prospect, a blockbuster of an account if you can get it, that you hesitate to call on–and put off and off and off–because you may get turned down.

When you face an unpleasant task, think of your self-image. The conflict between the right thing to do (call on Mr. Nasty, call on Mr. Big) and the easy thing to do (avoid Ms. Nasty, avoid Mr. Big) is yours entirely. How would a sales person with a positive self-image handle this?

For some backup support, take a sheet of paper and draw a line down the middle. On one side, write down all the reasons you can think of for making those calls now. On the other, write down all the reasons for procrastinating. When you weigh one side against the other, chances are that you will make those calls activity targets and reap the rewards.

Activity Target Guidelines

- **Take 10 to 20 minutes every day to work on activity targets.**

- **Daily targets are a must to sustain motivation.**
  They can be factions of your weekly or monthly targets. For example, if a target is to gain 20 referrals in the upcoming month, that translates to targets of five referrals a week, one a day.

- **Keep a written record of your progress.**
  This puts more fun in the game and it is easier to get psyched up when you work with a score card.

- **Maintain discipline.**
  Do not allow yourself to fall so far behind that you must depend on a blitz to hit your target.

- **Be sure that each target is specific, including the time frame to get it done.**
  A target should never be considered if I get a chance project.

- **Be sure that each target is a challenge worth pushing for.**
  It should never be an exercise for its own sake; if it is, you are just fooling yourself. There must be a clear payoff. Nothing else will motivate you.

Overcoming Slumps

Slumps are always bad, but they are not always the same. They are different things to different victims.

To some people, a slump means the bottom has fallen out:

> Everything I do is wrong. Every call I make is bad news. Nothing works anymore.

To some, it means there is a drought:

> I cannot even buy or steal a sale lately. There is nothing out there.

To some, it is discrimination:

> They are killing me. All I hear is no, no, no.

If you have never been in a sales slump, you just have not been in the business long enough. Slumps happen and because they can destroy motivation, you should know how to overcome them. But first, it is important to realize that success and slumps go together and slumps happen only to successful people (the others would not know the difference). Here are some reasons why slumps occur:

1. **The drive to succeed is all-consuming.**

   It is possible not only to be psyched up but to be psyched out–to run around selling at such a furious pace that good practices are cast aside. The effects? The result is overselling, under-servicing, quick shuffling of customers, too many complaints, a reduction in old-account business, new-account cancellations and–the last straw–an inability to sell or satisfy anyone. This is characteristic of the sales person for whom the bottom has fallen out. He had been overextending for so long that a slump was inevitable.

2. **The drive to succeed is in remission.**

   Complacency has crept in, but the sales person either does not know it or does not see it that way. When things still were going well, this sales person began to cut back–just a little here and there–on time spent where best spent, on effort expended, on enthusiasm and on concern for customers. Shortcuts replaced basics. Phone calls were returned a day late. New leads were handled by mailing the prospect a brochure. Then one day, out of nowhere, a slump struck. This is the sales person who has walked himself into a drought.

3. **The drive to succeed is struck down by mysterious forces.**
   These forces include luck, fate or the breaks. All of them are bad.
   Victims of this type of slump often attribute it to an event or a time of
   the year. For example: It all began when I lost that Smith account or I
   do not know why everything started to come apart right after Easter.
   From that point on, the sales person is convinced that until something
   changes, there is not much she can do about the slump. This is the
   sales person who feels helpless because of mysterious forces totally
   beyond her control. But in reality, the person has written her own
   script and then played it out.

Slump Factors: Drift and Depression

When you fall into a slump, you are not really sure what happened, no
matter what your personal theory. Once you begin to slide–and it sometimes
happens after losing a big sale or an account–you get depressed and suddenly
nothing is normal. Then you are not surprised when you continue to have
problems in selling. After all, you are in a slump.

Those setbacks or other factors that may have triggered the slide are almost
always of your own doing. That does not mean you were not trying your
best. As you understood it, you were trying your best. At that time, your
drive to succeed had gone off track you drifted away from the hard basics of
salesmanship. That drift led you right into a sales slump depression locked
you into it.

Depression-Fighting Tactics

When the frustration of not doing well turns into depression, you lose your
desire to sell. Depression hurts your ability to think clearly and make good
choices; it can turn an optimist into a pessimist. Because depression and
motivation do not mix, you need to charge up again. Here are some steps
to take:

1. **Discuss your feelings with someone.**
   Tell your manager, or a peer whom you respect, that you are having
   a problem, not because you are looking for advice, but to unburden
   yourself. The other person is likely to understand and to confirm that
   she has been through the same thing at some time.

2. Analyze our rejections.

After a turndown, take a few minutes to review what happened between you and the customer. Was this a suspect whom you never really qualified as a prospect? Did you take the time to probe current needs for product fits? Did you really listen to the customer? Did you give up at the first objection?

If you feel that you did a good job despite the rejection, so be it. You cannot make every sale. But you can learn something about yourself after each rejection and that is a plus if you take the time to analyze it.

3. Call on someone you do not care for–a crank, a pest, a loudmouth.

This is a challenge to get your juices flowing again. Nice guys would not help you here; picking up an order from a nice guy or an easy touch would not make a dent in your depression. Go for the challenge and for a feeling of accomplishment: Sell someone you just cannot stand!

4. Do something you do not have to.

You do not have to ask your boss to make some calls with you. You do not have to attend a sales training session. You do not have to set up a sales call for 8 a.m. And you do not have to spend a day prospecting. But there can be much satisfaction in doing something no one asks of you. More satisfaction means less depression and a more positive self-image.

5. Do not take days off.

You do not need the guilt. Work your way out of the blues you are experiencing. If you cannot push yourself to go out and sell products, get on the phone and sell appointments.

SELF-TEST NO. 1: PREFERRED ANSWERS

How do you feel about yourself? Each preferred answer is followed by a booster and a deflator. The booster is an example of the kind of thinking or action that strengthens your self-image; the deflator is the kind that weakens it. Understanding the difference between the two is especially important whenever your answer differs from the preferred answer.

1. I weigh my accomplishments against my expectations. True.
    Booster: You have clear, specific expectations and are most satisfied when your accomplishments meet those expectations.
    Deflator: You feel that any accomplishment is adequate, for example: Any sale is better than no sale.

2. I am easily upset. False.

    Booster: You are not readily thrown by the actions of others or by events out of your control; you are not destroyed by put-downs.

    Deflator: You are defensive, quick to take offense, or both.

3. My job is routine. False.

    Booster: You make demands of your job; you apply creativity to be sure that the job is not routine.

    Deflator: You label your work as routine and shape your activities to fit the label; you are reluctant to take risks.

4. I tend to push problems aside. False.

    Booster: I go after problems quickly.

    Deflator: I shelve problems as long as possible.

5. I enjoy being friendly. True.

    Booster: You tend to be outgoing, open and easy to talk to.

    Deflator: You tend to be cautious, reactive or, as a cover, blustery.

6. I shy away from the unfamiliar. False.

    Booster: You welcome the untried, the new.

    Deflator: If it is unfamiliar, you assume it would not work—or you are not sure you can cope.

7. I can laugh at myself. True.

    Booster: You are unafraid to laugh.

    Deflator: You are careful with laughter.

8. Bad news puts me in a bad mood. False.

    Booster: You are quick to recover from setbacks; you do not dwell on bad news.

    Deflator: You are easily depressed; you believe in luck and feel victimized by it.

9. Some people intimidate me. False.

> Booster: You refuse to be intimidated; you hold your position.

> Deflator: You can be intimidated by anyone who kicks up a fuss.

10. Some people take up too much of my time. False.

> Booster: You are a sharp manager of time; you would not let anyone mess with yours.

> Deflator: You are passive while others dribble away your time.

11. I often think about better ways to do things. True.

> Booster: I focus on improvement.

> Deflator: I focus on survival.

12. I hide my feelings from others. False.

> Booster: I show myself as I am.

> Deflator: I often hide my real self.

13. I am not easily or often fooled. True.

> Booster: I see through smoke screens.

> Deflator: I buy just about any story.

14. I make changes when I have to. True.

> Booster: I will junk the tried-and-true if I find a better way.

> Deflator: I am a follower; I will change only after others have.

15. I can be nasty when I have to. False.

> Booster: I remain civil under pressure.

> Deflator: I am unpredictable under pressure.

16. I think other people are as good as I am. True.

> Booster: I treat others as equals.

> Deflator: I feel that some people are either better than or not as good as I am.

17. I worry about failing. False.

> Booster: I concentrate on succeeding.

> Deflator: My primary objective at all times is to ward off failure.

SELF-TEST NO. 2: PREFERRED ANSWERS

Are you likely to excel? Check out how your attitudes stack up against the preferred answers.

1. A lot of money can be made in sales.
   Yes. If you do not believe the money is there, you will not make it. Your attitude toward money has to be that (1) it is available and (2) you can get it.

2. I prefer a straight salary so I can better plan my life.
   No. Compensation plans are important and most important of all is that you be satisfied with the plan your company offers. Nevertheless, the attitude of commission salespeople is: The sky is the limit. If you prefer straight salary, then that is the limit.

3. If I were a smoother talker, I could earn more money.
   No. You earn your living talking and that is a skill that can always be improved. But smoother talker, fancier dresser, better looking, taller–no. If it seems to you that certain physical attributes of other salespeople give them a selling edge over you, then you are selling with a second-echelon attitude.

4. I like being on my own.
   Yes. A No answer suggests a mind-set that is more compatible with inside sales than outside sales.

5. I do not think I get much respect being a sales person.
   No. This is probably the most important statement of the 12. Your attitude toward your job is linked to the measure of respect you think you are getting because of it. That includes respect from family, friends and customers. If you do not think your profession is one that merits respect, you are in trouble–both on and off the job.

6. I wish I had a nicer clientele to call on.
   No. If you answered Yes, the trouble with your clientele is that people are tough, smart and demanding. If you said No, people are also tough, smart and demanding. Your answer shows a difference not in clientele, but in attitude–yours. It can make a big difference in your success.

7. I learn more about people all the time.
   Yes. You can learn all there is to know about a product or service but not about people. No two are alike is a healthy attitude to take toward prospects and customers.

8. I am tired of people pleading poverty.
   No. No money to buy is the king of junkyard objections. If your attitude toward that is: I am tired of hearing it, you have been motivationally derailed and are probably buying objections that are pure fabrications.

> 9. I lose more sales because of price than any other factor.
>   No. Salespeople who believe that their products or services are overpriced sell with a negative, even destructive, attitude. The best thing to do in such cases is to get out.
>
> 10. Most of the sales leads I get are worthless.
>   No. To work sales leads for your profit, you have to be an active optimist: Every lead is a gem until I prove it otherwise.
>
> 11. I know there is a need for what I do.
>   Yes. No matter what you sell, your attitude has to be I am doing something useful. Without that attitude you are selling for money alone and customers will see right through you.
>
> 12. I know my business from A to Z.
>   Yes. Knowledge energizes attitude. There is no substitute for the confidence you gain from knowing that you have the answers.

IS A SALES FORCE WAITING IN THE WINGS?

Your salespeople know that an effective sales person is more than just an order taker. But do your sales-service telemarketers also know that? If they merely record orders that customers call in, they are missing an opportunity to contribute—and you also are missing out. Here is how you can help your sales-service staff make a greater contribution:

- **Point out the position of power they occupy.**

  They may not realize how far ahead in the sales process they already are. Salespeople expend enormous amounts of time and effort prospecting, qualifying and making appointments. Yet sales-service people have already pre-qualified those calling them. "So 80 percent of the work has already been done," says an office products regional sales manager. "Get that message across and you begin to create a sales person."

- **Make the job clear.**

  Sales-service people often consider a conversation closed after noting an order. But you can teach them to slide into a sales presentation: Thank you and by the way…Then, give them an understanding of sales strategy, as well as the specific product sales you are emphasizing. Much of this material can be scripted and hung on the wall in front of the staff to serve as a reminder and be used verbatim.

- **Keep up the training.**

  A series of training sessions to get the sales effort under way is bound to be effective and show up in your sales curve. But that graph will trail off unless you stay on top of the operation.

  "The more training we give them," says the office products manager, "the more sales they will produce." But reminders must be ongoing. The most effective way to ensure they are continuous is to assign a full-time manager to the sales-service group. The manager's salary or bonus should be covered by the additional sales that are generated.

- **Stress that no will not hurt them.**

  That is the same lesson you have taught so many times to your field people. The sales-service people have to learn it, too. Although no may bruise their egos from time to time, they will have no literal black-and-blue marks at day's end. What they will have is sales—if they understand that they cannot sit and wait for the customer to ask them for the order.

- **If they act like salespeople, treat them that way.**

  Why should your sales-service people bother to expend the extra effort to sell? What is in it for them? Why not recognition, trophies, their names in boldface in the house newsletter, bonuses—whatever you use to reward your dedicated sales force. If they like the rewards, they will get you more sales.

How to Tell Your Team: Shape Up!

A few years ago, former IBM chairman John Akers, distressed by his company's declining market share and plunging earnings, read the riot act to managers. His remarks, leaked to the media, were widely reported. One of his most quoted exhortations: "I used to think my job as a rep was at risk if I lost a sale. Tell them theirs is at risk if they lose."

When there has been a long losing streak, the boss, much like an athletic coach, must assemble the team for a shape-up talk. Some observers criticized the way Akers handled that meeting, however and said it would cause him to lose people's respect and support.

How would you handle such a situation? If, for example, your sales team's performance is below par in some way and you are certain it could be better, what would be the most effective way to bring about improvement?

Should people be pep-talked or reprimanded? Will anyone be singled out for criticism? Should there be ultimatums? Are jobs on the line?

Such a meeting can be even more difficult for a manager than for a company chairman. The manager is feeling the pressure from above. Things must change and that is what the meeting is all about. And like players on any losing team, everyone knows it.

Here are some ideas to help you handle this particularly difficult kind of meeting:

- **Come in with specific recommendations.**
  Unless you are prepared to introduce some change in procedure, rules, account or territory management or whatever, the meeting will have no core. People need to have confidence that you know what to do. The specifics you bring to the meeting will provide that confidence, whereas an open forum probably will not. Besides, without something solid to build on, you may find yourself drawn into a pep talk, reprimand or both—and you will generate much heat but little light.

- **Give salespeople the opportunity to add refinements.**
  You are not about to have your new procedure knocked down, of course, but someone may have a suggestion that strengthens it. After you outline the procedure, invite comments. Be clear about the kind of suggestions you are after: I welcome any ideas that might add to the success of this new procedure. And do not let anyone wander off the subject.

- **Keep the tone of the meeting strictly business.**
  The meeting need not be grim, but it needs to have some bite. It will not for long if it is punctuated with humor that threatens to run the meeting off track, for example, someone's funny put-down of an idea. (It is OK, however, to tolerate a humorous remark by a person obviously trying to alleviate the tension.) One way to close the door on humor is by not responding to it. Another way, if you need to take a firmer stand, is to say, in an even voice: This is a very serious situation.

- **Address your comments to the group as a whole.**
  Do not single out individuals for criticism. Do not point to an exception for praise. Your overriding objective is to pull the team together, not fragment it. The only important point as far as this meeting goes is the change or changes you will implement as a result.

- **Tell the group exactly what you expect.**
  Once you present your recommendations, clarify the way you want them implemented. Provide timetables, if applicable. Focus on the results you want. Make it plain why you know they are achievable–why, in fact, they must be achieved. If you get no disagreement on these points, you should consider that you have agreement. You should even say so and end on that note, leaving no uncertainties for anyone.

FOSTER YOUR TEAM'S DEVELOPMENT

A recent study found that many people leave a job not because they are dissatisfied with pay or conditions, but because they feel they are no longer developing. Field coaching is the single best tool for developing your staff, but you cannot be out there every week with every sales person. Supplement your coaching with some or all of the following. The results will be increased job satisfaction and better productivity. An added bonus: It will not take much of your time.

Books

There is a constant stream of new publications aimed at motivating, improving self-esteem, developing good work habits, sharpening sales skills and understanding and dealing with customers. These books are reviewed in such publications as *Selling Power* and *Sales & Marketing Management*. Recommend appropriate titles to salespeople. For example, a representative who is having trouble getting appointments might benefit from reading Art Sobczak's *How to Sell More in Less Time with No Rejection*. Tell him why you think he will find it helpful and ask him to focus on the sections that address openings and appointment making. Make it clear that reading the whole book is not necessary.

Audiotapes and CD's

These range from 20-minute rah-rah sessions designed to rev-up motivation to multipart programs on understanding customers and improving selling skills. Salespeople can listen to them as they drive from call-to-call, a big advantage given their crowded schedules. New titles are mentioned and advertised in sales publications, *Training* magazine and a plethora of catalogs, direct mail pieces and Internet sales ads.

Videotapes and DVD's

Chances are you have used a few of these for group training. Loan out appropriate segments for individual representatives to review. Then do a bit of role-playing with them the next time you field-coach to reinforce what the video demonstrated. Again, direct mail and the sales and training publications will alert you to what is out there.

Seminars

Look for programs designed to develop new or needed skills or inform your people about areas of opportunity. To pick the right ones, review the brochures to see what the seminar covers, how long it lasts, who the leader is, the target audience, the maximum number of participants per session and whether participants will be given manuals or other materials to take home. Take-home materials help retention. Also, check references. Call sales managers whose reps have attended the seminar. Ask them how their staff are using the program materials rather than how good they thought it was.

Memo

If you have the funds, set up a small library of books, audiotapes, DVD's, CD's and videos. Loan them out as needed to supplement your field coaching. If you hold regular sales meetings, you may want to ask the borrower to share a key suggestion or idea from the material or lead a discussion on it. Not only does this guarantee that the representative will review the material, but it ensures that all your people will benefit.

GROW YOUR PEOPLE VIA PLAN-AND-REVIEW SESSIONS

Staff development is a field manager's No. 1 responsibility. Monthly one-on-one plan-and-review sessions can go a long way toward helping you coach and support your salespeople as you would probably like to do if you only had the time. Including preparation time, such meetings take only 1 to 2 hours per sales person a month. You will find that the payoff far exceeds your investment of time.

In plan-and-review sessions, you and the sales person thoroughly review her achievements in the past month and discuss her goals for the coming month. The major objectives are to provide information, offer her support and help you reach your management goals by monitoring the quantity and quality of the sales person's selling activities. The only prerequisite is an activities tracking system. Once you have one in place and you have gained the cooperation of your sales staff, you are ready to go:

- **Prepare your people.**
  Call a meeting to explain the concept, answer questions and sell the benefits: better support leading to more effective selling and increased earnings. Wrap up by asking each person to give the system his best shot.

- **Prepare for each session.**
  This is a two-way street. The representative should give you his activities report prior to the session and be prepared to review the last month's activities with you, especially any problems he has encountered. Review the activities report and prepare questions to ask the representative. Also, consider what questions you would ask if you were the sales person. That way, you will have answers ready.

- **Kick off the session.**
  Start by asking the representative to review his past month's activities and results. Assist by asking probing questions to get him to analyze his work. For example: How were you able to make two more proposals this month? or Were there any common factors in the presentations that did not close?

- **Discuss successes and shortfalls.**
  Stress the positives first, then probe for the causes of problems. Generally, these will fall into two categories: inadequate skills or poor time management.

- **Ask the representative for solutions.**
  What do you think we can do to solve this problem? Discuss this until you agree on a specific course of action, one that focuses on measurable activities.

- **Review the representative's plan for the coming month.**
  Focus on key accounts, the close forecast and territory planning. Agree on the specifics of the plan. Let the representative know that he can use you as a resource, whether for advice, as a sounding board, for pep talks or as a liaison with home office personnel.

- **Ask for the representative's commitment and set a date for your next plan-and-review meeting.**
  You want the sales person to commit to the plan and problem-solving action, for example, to use a particular strategy to land a major account, to review a videotape on closing skills and to turn in call reports on time.

- **After the session, list what went well and what areas were problematic for you.**
  Then develop strategies for improvement. Do not expect your first sessions to be effortless. Plan-and-review sessions take time to master. But with practice, you will soon join an elite group: the fraction of sales managers who really nurture their team's development.

Observation

If you manage a large number of salespeople or a far-flung division, quarterly sessions may be more practical.

TAKE SOME OF THE PAIN OUT OF COST CONTROLS

Cost controls almost always cause resentment–mainly because they are often seen as a management whim rather than a necessity. To get your salespeople's cooperation and maintain morale during a period of belt tightening:

Include Salespeople in the Bigger Picture

Show them why the move is justified. Salespeople are bound to be resentful when told, for example, that they cannot write orders unless the customer can pay within 30 days. All they see is the sales they will lose. But if they are told that the tougher credit terms are necessary to improve cash flow–and that the firm's very survival is at risk–they are bound to be more cooperative.

Take Your Own Resentment to Your Boss, Not Your Salespeople

If you think a policy will hurt sales, do not commiserate with your salespeople. That will make you one of the guys in the short-term but will weaken company morale in the long run. Instead, let your boss give you the big picture and you may change your mind. If you still feel that the cuts will hurt sales and morale, draft a memo outlining why–in dollars and cents–management might want to rethink specific cost-control measures. Include any alternative suggestions you may have and send your memo to the appropriate person(s) at headquarters, with a copy to your boss.

How to Shore Up Morale during Layoffs

We are repeatedly reminded that downsizing occurs even in a healthy economy. If you are dealing with cutbacks in your firm, these steps will help boost your morale as well as that of your salespeople:

1. **Talk to managers outside your company who have also had to fire people.**
   Why people outside your company? Because conversation with colleagues in your firm can turn into a gripe session that resolves nothing. Outsiders can serve as a support group and help you talk through some of your problems and frustrations.

2. **Focus on the people left behind.**
   Call them together and explain what has happened and why. Reassure them about the future of the company and welcome their suggestions for making operations more efficient.

3. **Visit with staff members individually.**
   Some will be angry at you. Let them vent those feelings. Understanding their worries will benefit you as a manager.

4. **Help your sales force get back on track by developing new goals.**
   A smaller sales force may mean new consolidated territories and thus better opportunities for those left behind. Emphasize those benefits to help salespeople focus on the job, rather than on their fears.

5. **Build trust in the firm.**
   "Level with people and they will level with you," says Dr. Bruce Baldwin, author of *It's All in Your Head: Lifestyle Management Strategies for Busy People*. For example, if your firm is in a financial squeeze, say so. Chances are that your honesty will spark a positive response. "Staffers may even urge voluntary pay cuts," Baldwin says.

6. **Encourage everyone's input.**
   When people feel they play a meaningful role in an organization, they are more likely to give their maximum effort. Baldwin advises managers to watch for warnings of potentially disastrous breaks in morale: a humorless office atmosphere, sudden increases in turnover and escalating complaints from the rank and file.

Practical Approaches to Problem Solving

Even when you institute the best hiring practices, training and motivational tactics, specific problem areas still arise. You will need to give your sales reps a primer on how to tackle them. In this section we explore some common problem situations that you can identify early on to minimize their negative impact on sales. Of course, the material that follows is not only essential for your salespeople, but it is a natural review for the sales manager himself.

How to Handle the Sales-Saturated Buyer

Of course, you know enough to focus your greatest efforts on buyers with the greatest potential. Unfortunately, you are not the only sales person who is that smart, which means that you and your sharpest competitors all are descending on certain key buyers. Every now and then, those buyers understandably begin to feel besieged and will tell one sales person: Try me another time. I have seen enough salespeople for 1 day. What should you do if you are the unlucky one who appears when the buyer has reached the saturation point? You are not going to give up, not when you are that close. Try these tactics:

- **Sympathize and stay awhile.**
  Acknowledge the person's problem and point out, in low-key fashion, that ultimately he will have to make a decision. "I let him know I really

appreciate where he is coming from," says a sales person for a diagnostic equipment firm. "His own time and the efforts of all the people he has seen cannot be dismissed lightly. But I also point out that I might be able to help him avoid making the wrong decision."

• Follow through on that theme.

Once you are on firm ground about the need to make a decision, hold that position. "It is logical for me to dig for the three or four major requirements that will make the decision the right one for the customer and for me, too," says a sales person for a health care products company. The diagnostic equipment sales person adds, "I let the buyer know when I am probing that I would appreciate spending a little time talking to him before he has to make a decision because our firm thinks it would benefit him to look at–and use–our products."

• Tighten the advantage, if you can.

If the person says that one of the features you offer is of particular benefit, or if you are able to infer that it is, press forward on that one. "The way the health care system works these days," says the health care products sales person, "very often the one factor that weighs most heavily–assuming we are at least even with the competition on product efficacy and performance–is likely to be price. So cost-effectiveness is a phrase that tends to grab them."

• Push other advantages, too.

"Every other sales person who talks to the buyer will tell the same feature-benefit story," says the diagnostic equipment sales person. "But in my business there is a lot of uncertainty about the service that some companies provide, so I emphasize ours. I make it clear that whatever kind of customer problem comes up, we handle it and quickly."

• Use your judgment on the close.

Because the customer already feels overwhelmed by a crowd of salespeople, it is essential that you tread lightly. This is one of the few times when it could be wise to take a call-back on what might normally be a one-call close. "If I know that too much has been coming at the buyer, the last thing I want to do is push too hard," says the diagnostic equipment sales person. "If he seems to be ready to go, I will try to close right there. But if I sense that the buyer is edgy enough to be antagonized by a strong close at that moment, I will hold off and set up a solid appointment not too far in the future. Then I will send him a thank-you note for my call, add any information he requested and close with, I will see you Tuesday, the day on which I am likely to get the order."

WHEN THE BUYER LIKES TO BARGAIN . . .

For some buyers, bargaining must be part of the process. This is especially true when big-ticket items are involved and the buyer will not make a decision until she is certain it is the best purchase and the best deal for the company. Bargaining also occurs with a buyer who believes it is important to win and sees a good decision as a personal victory.

Because ordinary closing techniques may fall short when a buyer is primed for a session of give-and-take, it is important to sharpen your skills as a negotiator. Here are some guidelines:

- **Prepare a detailed proposal.**

  Specifics are easier to negotiate than generalities. They give the buyer opportunities to agree, partially agree or disagree, point by point. This enables you to answer objections as they arise and move toward the close in increments. It also lets you know where you stand every step of the way.

- **Use a negotiator's approach.**

  This means putting your offer on the table: Mr. Blaine, here is what we are prepared to do…Spell out costs, terms, delivery, guarantees—all the key specifics of the sale. The next move is the buyer's.

- **Retain some bargaining chips.**

  Include in your proposal some items that can be used as bargaining chips once the negotiations begin. The buyer will probably have some chips, too. For example, she may complain about price at first but then use it as a give-back later on. Time your concessions and trade-offs so that you present them at the most effective times. Do not offer them before they are needed.

- **Focus on areas of agreement.**
  Each time the buyer accepts part of your proposal that is an area
  of agreement. Go over the points with the buyer, one by one, to
  emphasize the similarities in your positions. It is easier to iron out
  differences once common ground has been established.

- **Identify the genuine objections.**
  Determine what the buyer wants that you cannot give. These are the
  true objections, not the ones being voiced just for the sake of argument.
  But instead of trying to overcome them, try to negotiate them. First,
  have a specific solution in mind. Then:

  - Play back the objection loud and clear. For example: Mr. Blaine,
    you say that no way will you pay shipping charges for deliveries.
    I can cut those charges in half for you by bunching our deliveries
    and shipping every other month instead of every month. This
    strategy allows the buyer to step back from an inflexible position by
    negotiating a way out. It is no longer an all-or-nothing, win-or-lose
    situation.

  - Know when to stop. Do not negotiate so hard that you put the
    other person on the defensive. That is likely to cause resentment
    and sabotage future sales, even if you manage to close this one.
    Remember: The most fruitful and mutually satisfying sales always
    are win-win situations.

Defend Yourself Against the Unfair Underbidder

Do you ever suspect that a competitor who underbid you–and thus won
an account–was bidding unrealistically low? Do you think of that as one
of those seriously unfair situations that is beyond your control? That is not
necessarily true.

Many companies rely on change orders, revisions in the specifications of
the original order, to raise their prices to a profitable level. Others simply
low-ball the bid and then present a higher figure on the invoice. If challenged,
they find some means of justifying the change. Thus, the prospect who went
with the competition to save money may have made a poor bargain. There
are steps you can take to verify that this is the case and then do something
about it.

1. **Review your lost orders.**

   Sort out those that were lost solely on the basis of price and look for patterns. Is one competitor consistently underbidding? Do any of your competitors get a last look and change their bids to win the contract? Which prospects encourage bidding wars between vendors?

   Note, too, how often customers who have strayed return to the fold. How many of them return because the price they were quoted was not the price they were charged?

2. **Run a check.**

   Do not hesitate to make a follow-up call on a prospect who chooses a lower bid. Ask specifically if the price he was quoted was the price he actually paid. The prospect who feels taken by your competitor will often be quite forthcoming. On the flip side, the prospect who is satisfied might give you some tips on areas where your company could save without cutting perceived value. For example, it is possible that certain services included in your price are not valued by the customer. Or he might feel that a middle-of-the-line component would serve his needs as well as the top-of-the-line component that is standard on your (higher-priced) offering.

3. **Capitalize on the information.**

   You now know what you are up against. If it is a question of over-engineering or servicing, pass the information along to headquarters. If it is purely pricing and a competitor's invoices are consistently higher than its quotes, you have a documented advantage. Use it. Show prospects actual proposals and invoices (cleared in advance with your customers or with names and identifying information deleted) to prove that you stand by your bids. Encourage them to ask the same of other vendors.

   To add to your ammunition, ask customers for letters contrasting a bad experience

Recommendation

Get in the habit of completing a lost order report for yourself on all sales that fall through. The report does not have to be formal or elaborate. But do record enough detail about why the sale was lost to allow you and the sales staff to analyze trends in the market.

Memo

Bad-mouthing the competition is a delicate art. Confer with your sales rep to be sure his strategy is in sync with company policy and will be viewed positively by the customer.

they had with a low-ball competitor with the satisfaction they have had dealing with your firm. Better yet, build a referral list of satisfied customers who are willing to talk to prospects who are weighing two or more bids.

How to Handle the Low-Priced Newcomer

When a newcomer tries to break into your market with a similar but lower-priced product or service, here are some steps you can take to protect your position:

- Expend little effort to win back price-sensitive small accounts that are not interested in the added value you offer. Focus instead on the loyal, small and midsize accounts and on infrequent users for whom price is not a big issue.

- Continue to work with your national accounts in a positive, rather than defensive, manner. Bear in mind that these accounts generally are your safest, both because they tend to have a stable nature and because insurgents usually are unprepared to play the national-accounts game. Only poor sales and marketing moves, such as benign neglect, will cause a national account to turn quickly to an unknown, price-oriented insurgent.

- Stay as flexible as you can in your dealings with all accounts in terms of both price and product offerings.

Avoid Account Losses: Heed the Warning Signs

I cannot believe we lost Acme. They were always such a strong account. There was never any clue that they were unhappy with us. Unless, maybe…. As much as it hurts when one of your salespeople loses an account, it is even worse if you suspect that there was a red flag you overlooked. The following customer behaviors might be early warning signs. If you spot any one of these, look into the matter fast:

An Account that Usually Pays Promptly Suddenly Slows Down

This could simply mean cash flow problems, which are not uncommon these days. But a slowdown in payment might also reflect dissatisfaction with your company. If this is the case, the account might not worry about late payments because it is about to switch to one of your competitors.

You Receive Routine Complaints, from the Customer's Vice President

In fact, these are not routine at all. Complaints might mean that the buyer has thrown up his hands after trying unsuccessfully to resolve problems with your company. Letters from a vice president might be signaling your last chance to save the account.

Your Calls Go Unreturned

If this happens often, or the person is repeatedly tied up when you phone, you could be seeing the smoke that signals a fire.

Your Service People Experience Long Waits

If your service people complain: They deliberately keep me waiting. Take notice. Possibly the word at that company is: Do not go out of your way for Acme, because they are getting ready to drop you.

Buying Patterns Change

A customer who usually orders substantial quantities but now places frequent minimum orders instead is signaling you. The account could be gradually shifting its business to a competitor who had been just a backup supplier.

To Rescue an Endangered Account:

1. **Make a personal call to the buyer without your sales person present.**

   People consider a visit from management an acknowledgment of their importance. Your call makes it clear that you value the account and want to do whatever is necessary to keep it.

2. **Call at the top, too.**

   If you do resolve the matter with the buyer, ask for permission to see the top management. You want to be sure she knows that you have reached an accord.

3. **Put your number where your mouth is.**

   Give the appropriate people at the account your direct telephone number so they can reach you quickly if things start to go sour again.

4. **Correct matters at home.**

   Whether the problem is with the sales person, delivery time, quality or something else, resolve it. Otherwise, you may find that the rule is: Two strikes and you are out.

Do You Invite Objections?

Do you find yourself dreading a certain objection or losing a much larger percentage of sales to that objection than your colleagues do? Paradoxically, you may be inviting the resistance you fear. Look for these symptoms and then use the tips that follow to modify your approach as well as that of your sales force.

1. You feel yourself tensing up when a customer approaches the problem objection–be it price, delivery time, power requirements, credit terms, lack of customization or service options.

2. You anticipate the dreaded objection and try to respond to it before the customer brings it up. Yet more often than not, it becomes a sticking point.

In the first case, the customer senses your tension and may well become wary. In the second, your attempt to refute a weakness that the customer has not even mentioned acts as a red flag. The customer senses a problem and then is not satisfied by your response to it. In both cases, the real problem is your lack of confidence in handling the objection.

Why are you having the problem? Rookie salespeople often have problems with certain objections because they have not learned how to handle them. They simply need to drill appropriate responses with their manager or a friend and then use them in the field until they are comfortable with them.

Experienced salespeople who encounter this problem will have to work a lot harder because it is generally their mind-set that is the problem. Whether or not you are consciously aware of it, you probably believe that your offering is weak in the area in question. So you have to overcome your own resistance before you can convincingly handle the customer's.

What you can do about it. First, do not anticipate the feared objection. If the customer does not bring it up, neither should you. Second, explore the area in question with an open mind. Why is your offering structured as it is? Why does your company insist on certain terms, use particular distribution channels or limit customer choice? When you know why something is the way it is, it is easier to accept. You may even discover that your company's offering is the best possible when all factors (target market, market needs, cost and so forth) are taken into consideration.

Third, role-play with your colleagues to come up with convincing responses to the objection. You play the customer and let a manager or a colleague play the sales person. Use a tape recorder to capture several sales calls in which you raise the problem objection. Then replay the tape and write down the specific words that convincingly handle the objection. Rehearse the response, then do another role-play session in which you play the sales person and respond to increasingly tough resistance.

Fourth, use those specific words in the field. After a few successes in handling the dreaded objection, you will find that you no longer fear it.

Memo

Be on the lookout for this problem when call reports reveal that a sales person is losing a disproportionate number of sales to a specific objection.

Coaching Salespeople Who Invite Objections

It is one thing to anticipate an objection. It is something else entirely to invite it and to cause a prospect to object. That happens when the sales person either has no faith in his ability to handle a specific objection or really believes that there is a flaw in the offering.

In either case, that lack of confidence somehow is communicated to the prospect. Perhaps the sales person tries to handle an objection by anticipating it but does it so unconvincingly that the prospect is alarmed and makes an issue of something that might never have been brought up otherwise. Or perhaps when it is brought up, the sales person reacts so strongly that his prospect becomes wary.

Even worse, a sales person may unconsciously introduce an objection as a throwaway line, such as: Do not worry about the linkage in this assembly. It is stronger than it looks. To spot this problem, you will have to watch the sales person handle objections on a number of joint calls. If you see that your sales person is communicating a lack of confidence, make note of the actual words used.

During a post-call coaching session, your first step is to point out to the sales person that he consciously or unconsciously believes there is a serious weakness in the sales proposition: We seem to run into that same price objection [or whatever it is] quite often. By my count, it is the decisive factor in almost every sale we miss. And I think you are leading with your chin…that you are asking for it.

Cite Their Actual Words

That probably will surprise most salespeople. So follow up with the convincer: their actual words. Let them hear how weak they sound, how they communicate their own lack of confidence to the buyer. Then tell them your plan for correcting this weakness in their presentation.

First, we have to change the words you are using, so you will not be inviting buyers to object on this point anymore. Second, I want you to understand why the price [or whatever] has to be what it is. Drill the sales person on the actual words and phrases to use when the objection does come up. Use role-playing so the sales person has free rein to express this frightening objection and also to see how effectively you can handle it.

As you work, write down the specific points you are making. Then, when you reverse roles, use those same points. Do not make it too rough at the start. Let the sales person gain a little confidence before you play the really tough buyer.

Following this, reach agreement that the sales person will try these techniques during every sales call for the next 2 weeks. Ask her for a progress report at the end of that time. If the sales person is still having trouble, you may want to provide visible proof that the feature in question is not a weakness and that there are solid reasons for its existence. This could mean a trip to the home office or plant to see the ingredients that dictate price or to talk to those who specify components so that the sales person can gain a better understanding of why things are as they are. If such a trip is impractical, the next best bet is to call on a satisfied user and ask why the account prefers your product.

Key Techniques for Handling Every Objection

You may be encountering more sales resistance these days. But no matter what objection a customer raises, no matter what responses you have at the ready, there are two techniques you should always employ. 1) Ignore them and you are in great danger of killing the sale. 2) Use them and you are on your way to success. What are they? Listening and questioning.

Listening is the most basic technique. Unless you begin by listening to and really hearing, what the customer is trying to tell you (or hide from you), you will not be able to decipher the message and the objection will stand.

Sometimes a customer will raise an objection to test your knowledge, sometimes to keep the upper hand and sometimes out of desperation– because his mind is wandering and the objection is a cover-up. If you pursue such objections blindly, you may detour the interview without ever getting to the real problem. In contrast, listening actively will bolster your own case.

Customers want time to build up their wall of resistance, just as you want time to tear it down. Their objections include opinions and feelings that they want you to show an interest in, not to short-circuit. If your response to an objection is off-center, you lose ground. The customer knows immediately that you were not listening, have not fully grasped the problem or do not have an answer and are being evasive. Any canned answer you may offer can fit no more than 99 percent of the objection and that is not enough.

A fully expressed objection can be a tip-off to a customer's real needs. Sometimes, if allowed plenty of leeway to express an objection, a customer will wander right into critical territory. For instance, the person opens with: I just will not deal with a company that I do not know and I am fed up with people who come in here with promises and then cause me grief because they can not deliver. Only by listening to this person from beginning to end is it possible to address the problem right on target.

Questioning is the only way to determine cause. Good questions get customers to reveal specifics and help you narrow down an objection to manageable size. Say, for example, the buyer examines a sample of your product:

> Customer: "I do not think it will hold up."
>
> Your question: "You do not think it is heavy enough or strong enough?"
>
> Customer: "The stuff we are using now is much heavier."

As a result of your questioning, you know you need to show proof that less weight does not mean less strength. Reducing an objection to a manageable specific also reduces the magnitude of the objection for the customer. After you ask: "Heavy enough or strong enough?" The buyer realizes that the objection is being halved because she has considered and made a choice. The buyer's uneasiness has been reduced. Thus, your presentation can be more focused.

How Are You Really Doing? Look behind the Numbers

In sales, the numbers tell practically all if you read them carefully. Trouble is, some managers look at the macro figures–overall sales to date, average margins on their various lines and overall sales ratios–and fail to spot early warning signs of trouble in the offing. To get an accurate picture of how you are doing, you have to look at the numbers behind the numbers: Results by individual sales persons and product line. Here are some areas to explore:

Sales

What is the spread of business? Are your top producers bringing in most of the business, thereby disguising the lagging results of 80 percent of your sales reps? Are most individuals meeting their sales goals? If not, how far short are they falling? Are sales of any one product or line conspicuously over or under goal? Why? Is it a hard sell? Is the compensation structure at fault? Have you failed to push the product or the line?

Margins

What percentage of your overall volume yields average or above-average profits for your company? How does this vary by individual sales representative? Are some reps meeting their volume goals by frequently cutting special deals that are only minimally profitable?

Sales Ratio

Check these ratios by individual sales rep: The average number of new contacts to qualified prospects; qualified prospects to presentations; presentations to closes; proposals to closes; new contacts to closes; overall sales calls to closes; and new accounts to total accounts. If a representative's ratios are higher or lower than average in any of these areas, find out why. A little coaching may help a sales rep bring up a low ratio, while a probe of why another's ratios are high may give you valuable ideas to pass along to the rest of your sales force.

Accounts

Do you have a healthy mix of large and small and old and new accounts? Or are a few large perennials responsible for most of your territory's volume? Are most new accounts either smaller or larger than the average established account? Again, check by individual sales representative, bearing in mind that some territories are more fertile than others. If new accounts are generally small, review the qualifying process your people are using. It may need tightening to ensure that they are not wasting their time on small fry when they could be pursuing the big fish.

Sales Rep Development

How many of your hires have become top performers? How many started out well but have not lived up to their initial promise? What percentage of the average salespeople you inherited when you were assigned to your current territory have improved their performance? Do you have a written plan for each representative whose performance is below par? Remember, the most important part of your job is developing sales talent.

Sales Rep Turnover

Some turnover is healthy. No turnover or a high turnover rate means you have problems. The latter may be a sign that you expect representatives to make it on their own, without coaching, or that you set unrealistically high goals. No turnover, on the other hand, may mean that you just cannot bring yourself to fire anyone, no matter how poor his performance. Keep in mind that everyone gets hurt that way: The poor performer is not given the needed push to seek work that he could do well; your other reps get less attention than they deserve; and you look bad because the laggard drags down your results.

Non-Sales Procedures

Are call reports submitted on time? Do you read them and give feedback? Are expenses within company guidelines? Is the collection rate acceptable? Do you have a system for handling customer complaints promptly and satisfactorily?

Recommendation

If your look at the numbers behind the numbers reveals problems that only upper management can solve, pass along your findings to your boss. For example, your salespeople may avoid selling a line because the commission structure discourages them from investing the time required to make a sale. Your feedback might be just what is needed to get upper management to remedy the situation.

Eliminate Non-buyers, Sharpen Your Qualifiers

Losing a sale to a competitor is bad enough. But losing a prospect to indecision is even worse. Why? Because it suggests that time was spent on a suspect with no potential. In this imperfect world, that will happen on occasion. But you can help your salespeople come close to eliminating non-buyers from their call reports. How? By sharpening their qualifying skills.

What is a qualified prospect? The first step in this process is to re-examine your company's definition of a qualified prospect. There is always the possibility that the old definition no longer works. To find out, put a hard-hitting analysis of lost orders on the agenda of your next sales meeting:

- First, reach a consensus on how the sales force defines qualified prospect. Write all the key qualifying factors on a flip chart for reference during the meeting.

- Next, have salespeople discuss their no decision cases in detail. The goal is to figure out what key qualifying factors were missing in each case. As you discover these, write them on another flip chart. When you finish, you will have a better idea of what seems to be going wrong.

- Then, ask the group to decide if it might be time to reconsider the original definition of a qualified prospect. If so, how should the definition be changed? If your people do not ask the hard questions, ask them yourself:

  Are we making it too easy for prospects to participate in our sales process?

  Are we going into companies at the wrong level of management?

  How can we be sure a prospect has the money before we do a complete survey and a 3-hour demo?

Build Qualifying Skills

No matter how tightly you define qualified, many salespeople will still shy away from asking the hard questions that might force them to eliminate a prospect. If they are still in the pipeline, there is always hope seems to be their attitude. Or, to put it another way, the lead is not dead until the prospect is. Getting salespeople past those roadblocks is an ongoing training and development challenge for most sales managers.

The first step in this segment is to help salespeople understand that it is just as important to eliminate unqualified prospects as it is to present proposals to qualified ones. The second step is to make them comfortable with the skills they need to become ace qualifiers. Role-plays based on their actual lost-order situations are an excellent way to do that. They allow your people to get used to asking direct (and possibly uncomfortable) questions about such key qualifiers as:

Need

Your present system seems perfectly adequate for your needs. Why do you not just keep it? What is there about that situation that makes you want to change? Why can you not just live with things the way they are?

Buying Authority

Who will be on the committee that reviews the proposal? May I meet with each committee member in advance so that I can better address their concerns in my proposal? May I have 10 minutes on the agenda of that meeting to present the technical information the committee will need to make the best decision? What would happen if you chose a system that the president had not seen and it turned out that she did not like it?

Money

Has money been budgeted for a new widget? What is your ballpark figure? Perhaps the best thing to do would be to check with the CFO first. I would be more than happy to be at that meeting if you feel it is appropriate. Would that help? If you decided you needed a new widget but the budget did not quite cover it, how would you find the extra money?

Time Frame

When are you planning to make a change? It will take about 30 days to complete a survey, conduct a demonstration and prepare a proposal. Will you be in a position to make a decision then? What time of year do you usually make decisions of this sort?

Observation

The combination of a tightly focused definition and hard-hitting, pointed questions should ensure that your salespeople get the greatest possible return on their investments of time and effort.

PAYMENTS OVERDUE? THESE TACTICS WILL HELP

If it is up to you to act as the collection agency for your own accounts, you may be reluctant to handle this less-than-pleasant task. If you approach each collection as a sale to be closed with firmness, but not hostility, you will experience less aggravation and a high success rate. Try these suggestions:

- **Arm yourself with information.**
  Walk in knowing exactly how much is owed and how long overdue it is. "I have all that information in front of me," a printing sales person says. "If I am calling on the phone, I also find out whom I am talking to first, so the buyer cannot tell me he is not here right now or just take a message."

- **Shed no tears over their sad tales.**
  If the customer rationalizes the failure to pay on the grounds that your company did something wrong, be polite, but do not buy it. The customer might suddenly remember, for example, that the quality really was not up to par or you were 4 days late on that last delivery–and so on. Remind her that you have never heard a word of complaint until now and then get back on track: "I tell them that if they expect our service and material when they want it, they have to pay within a reasonable period of time," a computer systems sales person says. "I am not sidetracked by any spur-of-the-moment beef."

- **Avoid the casual approach.**
  "This is not a by-the-way call," the printing sales person says. "I am direct and to the point–no small talk. Otherwise, I will never collect a penny."

- **Use a silent close.**
  In this situation, silence can literally be golden. "I just say you are 60 days overdue. And then I shut up," the printing sales person says. "Usually, the first one who talks loses in these situations, so I wait. That makes the person uncomfortable and usually draws an immediate offer."

- **If silence fails, speak right up.**
  "I ask for the money, making no bones about it," the computer systems sales person says. "At worst, I go for a commitment, an amount and date." Or, the printing sales person says, "I try something like asking for half now and we will set up the rest in three payments–or whatever I think I can get. I hardly ever leave without some money."

- **Sound the alarm.**

  If you are genuinely concerned that payment may not materialize, let your manager know. Then the home office can decide if the account should be put on c.o.d. or cut off altogether. Remember, if the account's not profitable, it is not an asset to you or your company. You are better off losing it before it costs you even more.

WHEN THEY WANT TO THINK IT OVER . . .

The last thing you want to hear from a prospect who needs your offering and has the money to buy it is that he wants to think it over. What is to think over? you want to holler. You have agreed that it could solve a problem for you. If you cannot move past this objection–by probing the reasons for the prospect's hesitation and trying to resolve lingering doubts–you might try giving the person a deadline. Here are some examples:

Price-Related Deadlines

I know that you want to make the right decision for your company, Ms. Jones. Let me remind you, however, that this price is guaranteed only until the end of the month, which is next Wednesday. Or, as I think I told you, this is a special offer, which we are extending only to customers who sign up for our service by the 15th. That gives us only 3 days to get you on line at this price.

Scheduling-Related Deadlines.

Ms. Wong, you have told me that the installation would have to be complete by Aug. 30 to ensure that your fall production would not suffer. We can work within that time frame, but we will need at least 45 working days to produce, ship, install and test. So to meet your timetable, we would need a signed contract by June 29th.

Training-Related Deadlines.

Of course, we cannot schedule the user training you say is essential for your people until we have a signed contract from you. We schedule our trainers on a first-come, first-served basis. Judging by the current schedule, I would say that if we have your order by next Tuesday, there

Caution

Link your deadlines to potential gain or loss for the prospect and use them only if they are real. The special must actually be ending; the price guaranteed only until the end of the month; the upfront time really 45 working days; the trainers really assigned on a first-signed, first-scheduled basis. If your deadlines are just ploys and the prospect finds that out (for example, by finally ordering three months later and getting the same or a better deal), you and your company will lose credibility.

will be no trouble scheduling your training when you said you would like it.

WHEN A PROSPECT WANTS YOU TO SWEETEN THE DEAL . . .

A recent New York State legal case highlights a sticky situation that salespeople encounter on occasion. A Digital Equipment Corp. sales person was charged with giving $13,000 in entertainment gifts to state officials who had computer-buying authority. Those officials later recommended or approved more than $10 million of purchases from Digital. State authorities called the gifts improper and said they compromised the buyer's objectivity. When Digital learned about the gifts, it dismissed the sales person.

Just because you would never consider making such an offer to a prospect does not mean you will not have to face the situation. What would you do if a prospect implied that some kind of contribution on your part would expedite an order? Here is how you can stick to your principles:

1. **Make your position clear immediately.**

   You do not have to show anger but leave no doubt about where you stand. A TV station advertising sales person says she occasionally encounters a prospect who asks for double billing as a way of pocketing the 50 percent co-op reimbursement the station pays. Depending on the individual, the sales person's response might be slightly humorous, firm, but never ever hinting that it would be acceptable under any circumstances. Naturally, this is a very delicate and tricky area—one that requires maturity and honesty. It also may mean that you will not get the business.

2. **Use your response to move smoothly to your next point.**

   "Explain that there is no play in our prices that will permit me to share our profits with them because we want to keep costs as low as possible in our very competitive industry," a computer software sales person says. Then he adds politely that ethics and the law are considerations, too; then I just go on selling.

3. A turndown will rarely lose you a sale.

Most of the time, the request or suggestion is only a trial close on the part of a petty thief. "I do not think that standing firm has ever cost me a sale," the software sales person says. Still, if the buyer is insistent even after you have refused to play, one way to get him to back off is to say: Well, I really do not know whether I have the authority to do this. But I could have my company president call yours to check it out. OK? You can imagine that such a response will put an end to such requests; they can only work if the conspiracy is tightly contained.

PROSPECT NOT INTERESTED? ASK HER WHY NOT?

It may be discouraging to hear, I am not interested, just when you thought you were about to close the sale. But it does not have to mean you will walk away empty-handed. Focus on the real objection and close on it instead.

The real objection? If you are a rookie who has not yet mastered the art of establishing need, you may be trying to close someone who cannot use your product. But there is a better chance that this no means that it is too expensive or not worth the price. In other words, you are facing a money objection decked out in fancy clothes.

Caution

If the request hits you unexpectedly, or if the buyer is asking for something that seems inconsequential, you might decide to do it just this once to get the creep off your back and never do it again. Do not take this approach. Once you show that you are willing to give even a little bit, the person will try to find out how much more you will give and you will be in for a long ride. The word will spread, too and every chiseler in the territory will be waiting to sandbag you.

How to counter with why not? The following dialogue illustrates how to close on the I am not interested objection using the why not approach:

Prospect: "No. I am not interested."

You: "Thanks for being direct, Mr. Millit. The last thing I want to do is waste your time. May I ask why you are not interested?"

Prospect: "It just is not for me."

You: "Is there something about the offer that turns you off?"

Prospect: "No. I am just not ready right now."

You: "Why is that, Mr. Millit?"

Prospect: "Well, for one thing, I do not have that kind of money to spend."

You: "May I ask how much you would be interested in spending for something of this quality?"

Prospect: "Hard to say. But I know I can not go that high."

You: "There are cheaper services on the market. We just do not provide them. [You go into a thorough review of features, benefits and exclusives.] You cannot get this kind of value, anywhere, for less money." [Silence.]

Prospect: "I believe you. But it is just too big an expenditure for us right now."

You [shifting to a savings close]: "Yes, it is a big expenditure. That is all the more reason to know exactly the kind of return this investment will bring. May I take just a minute more of your time, Mr. Millit?"

Prospect: "I guess so."

You: "Let us go over the savings you can expect…[You attach dollars to factors such as ease of installation and operation, reduced maintenance, higher productivity and so forth—all the pluses of the offering that pay back over time.] What is more, we can arrange financing terms that mean your actual monthly expenditures will increase by only $50 and for only nine months. After that, you will be saving a minimum of $125 per month compared with your current outlays. In short, I think this is an investment that will pay off for you for years to come, Mr. Millit. Do you see my point?"

Prospect: "I suppose so."

You: "I need your approval right here." [Silence.]

Observation

This approach will not work every time, but it will help you close some customers. If you hear that they are not interested often, however, chances are that you are not qualifying effectively for need. Give your sales reps help in honing their qualifying skills.

YOU MAY STILL HAVE A SHOT AT THE ONE THAT GOT AWAY

Unless you are the rare sales person with more qualified prospects than you need, you cannot afford to pass up accounts that bought from you and paid up in the past but dropped you at some point because of a dispute, a missed delivery or some other problem. It is well worth the effort to approach an account you had and lost.

But they dropped you, you protest. True, but it is possible that things have changed. Any one of the following changes could give you a shot at getting the business back.

- **Changes at the account.**
  The buyer at the time the account was lost may have moved on. Even if the new person knows why your firm lost the business, she may be willing to listen and give you another chance. After all, this is not the person who rejected you or your firm. In fact, even an injured buyer may be willing to give you another chance. "I find that sometimes a client who was really upset with me or my company, for whatever reason, finally simmers down," an office products sales person says. "The client listens to me, decides that it was not the end of the world and I am back. Also, if I have got a good idea, almost anyone is willing to listen, regardless of past experience." And getting people to listen is the first step on the road to sales.

- **Changes at your company.**
  Possibly the perpetrator of the crime—missed delivery, tardy service, billing errors—is a particular operating manager whose methods turned off many accounts. That might ultimately have led to his dismissal. A statement such as: "We saw that we were having a problem, so we have replaced that manager and things have really turned around" may be all that you will need to get the buyer to reconsider.

- **Changes in focus.**
  If a former customer can be persuaded that your company's approach to its own business is now more to her liking, the person might relent. A sales person for a maker of highway construction equipment, which is a subsidiary of a larger one, recalls a problem he ran into a few years ago. The parent firm, which was then the direct seller of a product line that the subsidiary now sells, abruptly pulled out of one market area, leaving its customers high and dry—and angry. Today, the subsidiary, which is a completely independent entity, is handling the line.

Now we go back to many former customers and make the case that we are a different company, despite our nominal tie to the parent," the sales person says. "Most important, we emphasize that this product and

Observation

One sales person says that even when he is not the guilty party, he will assume responsibility just to get things moving again. He will take the blame, but ask to be heard this time. Let me show you that I can do the job for you. One reason that this works is that I always try to keep up some contact with a lost client. It might be a note or a phone call asking how are things going? The idea is that communication between us is never totally severed. After all, few people bear grudges forever.

market are critical to our well-being and we intend to stay with it for a long time." It is a hard sell, he admits, but he has been able to persuade some former customers to return to the fold.

- **Changes in you.**
  Perhaps you were young and green and blew the business all by yourself. Going back with a mea culpa, but the I am smarter now argument will convince many people to give you another chance.

TOO MANY CALLS TO CLOSE A SALE?

Some of your more experienced salespeople may have developed a feel for the number of calls they will need to make to close a sale with a particular type of prospect. For example, a sales person might refer to a two-call close, meaning that in theory the sale can be made in two calls–perhaps one call to generate interest and leave a sample or literature and a second call to confirm the prospect's satisfaction and write up the order. For other prospects, a sales person might speak of a one-call or a three-call close. Few salespeople–except those selling big-ticket items–like to admit it when they have more than a four-call close.

The words, in theory, are the problem. It is possible to close sales in four calls or fewer and that is done often enough to make it seem reasonable for salespeople to do it every time. Practice, however, does not always match theory. In most cases, the two- or three-call rule of thumb is only an ideal to shoot for rather than an everyday occurrence.

How many calls do you really have to make? Surveys have shown that it can take as many as five calls to close a sale. On the front end, the need for that many calls could reflect difficulties with missed appointments or locating the decision maker. On the back end, there could be problems with handling stalls and objections.

This variety of possible reasons simply shows that regardless of what theories or rules of thumb might suggest, the sales person should make as many calls as are necessary to close a prospect who has true potential. That is, the sales person's approach should be one of polite persistence.

What is polite persistence? We think this term is best illustrated by a story (perhaps invented by a sales person) that we have heard from several sources. It concerns a new sales person for a large distributor who was given the assignment of trying to open a number of accounts that had been lost for one reason or another.

On his first visit to the purchasing department of the XYZ Company, the sales person signed the log, presented his card to the receptionist and waited. Twenty minutes later, an embarrassed secretary appeared and announced: Mr. Jones asked me to give you this. It was the sales person's business card–torn into pieces.

Two weeks later, the sales person returned the same scenario was played out–his card was returned in shreds. He made two more visits with the same results. On his fifth visit to XYZ, the routine was almost the same, but there was one crucial difference: The card he presented was printed on aluminum. Almost immediately, Mr. Jones himself appeared in the waiting room. The sales person left that day with a small order from his new account.

Observation

Of course, the time comes when any sales person has to cut bait instead of waiting for the bite that will never come. Be sure that your people are clear about the difference between dropping by to shoot the breeze with people who will not buy and polite persistence in the pursuit of valid objectives and true sales potential.

How Do You Rate as a Sales Manager?

Getting a solid fix on your strengths and weaknesses as a sales manager would undoubtedly help you become more effective, improve personnel development and sales revenues in the process—maybe even put yourself in line for a promotion. Trouble is, those who have the best fix on your management abilities report directly to you. They are unlikely to jeopardize the relationship by pointing out areas in which they think you need to improve. Moreover, you would need feedback from each of them to get a rounded picture of your skills. Still, if you are willing to accept such direct feedback graciously, you can get it.

Start by asking a third party—for example, your boss or someone in human resources—to help you gather the information in a ratings survey. You want someone who is willing to mail out questionnaires and tabulate the results, thereby assuring anonymity to the participants. The person you are working with has to be willing to put in some time because you will need to know all the ratings you receive for each question separately.

It is up to you to come up with questions that will allow your salespeople to rate your skills as well as to devise a rating scale. We suggest a scale from 1 to 5, with 1 being poor and 5 being excellent.

Jack Snader, CEO of Systema, a company that specializes in skills assessment and professional development, suggests that you ask your people to rate you in such areas as goal setting, planning, training, communication and time management. For example, on a scale of 1 (poor) to 5 (excellent), you could ask: How well do I:

SELF ASSESSMENT

___ Discuss goals and quotas with you to be sure they are clear?

___ Encourage you to express your opinions and participate in decisions?

___ Answer questions about compensation policies, products or selling skills?

___ Systematically plan and organize the sales effort?

___ Coach you to help you improve your performance on the job?

___ Let you know where you stand?

___ Stress the need to get things done on time?

___ Keep track of your performance in terms of sales and skills?

___ Develop your self-confidence in your ability to plan your own work?

___ Praise good sales efforts and give credit where it is due?

___ Make it easy for you to say what is on your mind?

___ Develop cooperation and a sense of loyalty among members of the sales group?

___ Build group motivation and morale?

You would also want to ask them:

___ What should I continue to do?

___ What should I stop doing?

___ What am I not doing that you think I should be doing?

Before you get any feedback, rate yourself by answering the questions you have posed. Then, once you get the feedback, compare the ratings with one another and with your own self-assessment. You will get a fairly accurate picture of not only your strengths and limits but also your blind spots, areas in which you think you are strong but your salespeople consider you weak. You will also probably discover areas in which you receive widely different ratings from various salespeople. That could signal the need to vary your approach when working with different people because what's effective with one may not work with another.

If it sounds like a fair amount of work, it is. But sales executives, such as Tom Heller, vice president of U.S. operations for Abbott Laboratories Diagnostic Division, say the effort pays off in increased sales. Abbott more than doubled its sales in 3 short years, Heller says, thanks in large part to a self-development effort by managers who asked sales representatives to assess their skills.

If you are willing to accept direct feedback graciously, you can get it.

You will get a fairly accurate picture of not only your strengths and limits but also your blind spots.

Appendix I
The Resources

Products and Services

There are many programs which assist sales managers, even the entire sales and marketing departments for that matter. One well-advertised program is called Salesforce.com. It is reportedly the worldwide leader in on-demand customer relationship management (CRM) services and software. It is said to have more than 550,000 subscribers at more than 27,000 companies worldwide. Among the features advertised for users are:

- lead management
- account management
- territory management
- contract management

The service comes with analytical and forecasting tools, including sales analytics, global forecasting, data management and a variety of dashboards. Company product information-including catalogs and other selling aids-can be integrated into the CRM system. For further information, free trial/demo and pricing, visit *www.salesforce.com*.

The Sales Company provides one-on-one training for sales professionals (sales consulting) as well as overall consulting concerning your sales program and strategies. For more information, visit *www.the-sales-company.com*.

There are any number of qualified, highly-respected national recruiting agencies that assist sales managers in finding and hiring the best, qualified salespeople for their particular industries. For example, SalesTalent offers services for both employers and salespeople looking for employment. For additional information, visit *www.salestalentinc.com*.

Vanguard Software offers the Vanguard Sales Manager which is a mobile field sales system, running on pocket PCs. It allows users to track customers and products, take orders and print invoices. Note that this is a company originating from the United Kingdom. For more information, visit *www. vanware.co.uk/*.

PointsPlan is a sales incentive program which can be purchased off the shelf, without extensive in-house customization. The developers offer the claim that sales managers can reduce their dependence on the human resource department to come up with an appropriate incentive program specifically for sales personnel. According to the company Website, PointsPlan is a hosted application that allows sales manager to award points to any positive performance-for sales, for online training, for surveys and for reaching specific sales targets. For more information, visit *www.pointsplan.com*.

Insidesales.com is an on-demand sales automation and customer management software which integrates a suite of sales and marketing tools, including lead management, analytics, dialers and voice messaging, among other features. The software is hosted online, so no IT commitment is required. For further information, visit *www.insidesales.com*.

Consulting

Topline Leadership, Inc. is one of many consulting and training companies which offer a variety of services for sales training as well as sales manager training. The training is delivered by seminars. There are a variety of articles and case studies on the site and this alone may be worth a visit. For additional information, visit *www.toplineleadership.com*.

Prime Resource Group is a management consulting firm specializing in sales and marketing management-especially for companies with complex sales. In addition, they offer sales training, marketing strategies and new product strategies. Several books are sold on the Website as well. For further information, visit *www.primesalesmanagement.com*.

Schneider Sales Management, Inc. is a consulting and sales training firm specializing in the financial services industry. The company's claim is that using their services will bring about a 300 percent increase in sales growth over industry averages (banks, savings and loans and credit unions). The site includes free content, including newsletters, articles and sales tips. Visit *www.schneidersales.com* for more information.

Books

There are some excellent additions to this book, emphasizing a variety of sales strategies and techniques, useful for both managers and their salespeople.

Among the titles, consider the following:

Getting into Your Customer's Head: 8 Secret Roles of Selling Your Competitors Don't Know, (Times Business/Random House).

Seven Secrets to Successful Sales Management: The Sales Manager's Manual, (CRC, 1997), available at *www.7salessecrets.com.*

Welcome to Sales Management: The First 90 Days and Beyond, (Authorhouse, 2004).

Sales Coaching: Making the Great Leap from Sales Manager to Sales Coach, (McGraw-Hill, 1996).

These books can be purchase at *www.amazon.com* and *www.barnesandnoble. com* as well as at major book retailers.

Websites

The U.S. Department of Labor is a rich resource about job classifications, salaries, qualifications for sales management positions, as well as employment outlook. Visit Bureau of Labor Statistics-Occupational Outlook Handbook at *www.bls.gov.*

CNN Money.com has some useful information about financial rewards and the future of sales management as a career. According to their data, sales management is the 5th of the Top 10 paying professions, averaging over $135,000 per year. For more information, visit *http://money.cnn.com/magazines/moneymag/bestjobs/snapshots/21.html.*

For additional information about human resource information, benefits and general employment issues which may be useful for sales managers, visit *www.allbusiness.com* and search for the human resource section of this Website.

Sales Management is a general reference Website for sales managers seeking a variety of products and services, from training to software. Visit *www.onlysalesmanagement.com* for more details.

Forms

The forms provided here are illustrative of what is typically used for new hires. Some forms may not be legally binding in your state, so some caution is required if you decide to use them.

Employment Application

Company policy offers equal employment opportunity to all qualified applicants without regard to race, creed, color, religious belief, sex, age, national origin, ancestry, physical or mental handicap or veteran status.

Date _____________

Name: Last ________________ First ____________ Middle _______

Address ____

City ____________________ State ________________Zip ______

Telephone (___) ___________ Social Security # ________________

Position applied for ____

How did you hear of this opening__________________________________

When can you start _____________ Desired Wage $ _____________

Are you a U.S. citizen or otherwise authorized to work in the U.S. on an unrestricted basis? [ ] Yes [ ] No

Are you looking for full time employment? [ ] Yes [ ] No

If no, what hours are you available? _________________________

Have you ever been convicted of a felony? [ ] Yes [ ] No

If yes, please fully describe the circumstances: _________________

____

____

Education: School Name and Location Year Major Degree

High School ____

College ____

College ____

Other ____

Do you have other skills, qualifications, or experience we should consider:

____

____

Employment History: (Start with most recent employer.)

Company name ____

Address ____

Telephone _________________________

Date Started ______ Starting Wage______Starting Position _________

Date Ended _______ Ending Wage ______Ending Position _________

Name of Supervisor ________________May we contact? [ ] Yes [ ] No

Responsibilities ____

____

____

____

Reason for leaving ____

____

____

____

Company name ____

Address ____

Telephone ____________________

Date Started ______ Starting Wage______ Starting Position __________

Date Ended ______ Ending Wage ______ Ending Position __________

Name of Supervisor ______________________ May we contact? [   ] Yes [   ] No

Responsibilities ____

____

____

____

Reason for leaving ____

____

____

____

Company name ____

Address ____

Telephone ____________________

Date Started ______ Starting Wage______ Starting Position __________

Date Ended ______ Ending Wage ______ Ending Position __________

Name of Supervisor ______________________ May we contact? [   ] Yes [   ] No

Responsibilities ____

____

____

____

Reason for leaving ____

____

____

____

Company name ___________________________________

Address ___________________________________

Telephone ___________________

Date Started ______ Starting Wage______Starting Position __________

Date Ended _______ Ending Wage ______Ending Position __________

Name of Supervisor __________________May we contact? [ ] Yes [ ] No

Responsibilities ___________________________________

____

____

____

Reason for leaving ___________________________________

____

____

____

Attach additional information if necessary.

I certify that the facts set forth in this application for employment are true and complete to the best of my knowledge. I understand that if I am employed, false statements on this application shall be considered sufficient cause for dismissal. This company is hereby authorized to make any investigations of my prior educational and employment history. I understand that employment at this company is "at will," which means that either I or this company can terminate the employment relationship at any time, with or without prior notice and for any reason not prohibited by statute. All employment will continue on that basis. I understand that no supervisor, manager, or executive of this company, other than the president has the authority to alter the foregoing.

Signature___________________________________

Date ___________________

Non-Compete Agreement

For good and valuable consideration the receipt of which is hereby acknowledged, _______________________________ (Employee), the undersigned Employee hereby agrees not to directly or indirectly compete with the business of ____________________________ (Company) and its successors and assigns during the period of employment and for a period of ____ years following termination of employment and notwithstanding the cause or reason for termination.

Employee shall not own, manage, operate, consult or to be employed in a business substantially similar to, or competitive with, the present business of Company or such other business activity in which Company may substantially engage during the term of employment.

Employee acknowledges that Company may, in reliance of this agreement, provide Employee access to trade secrets, customers and other confidential data and good will. Employee agrees to retain said information as confidential and not to use said information on his or her own behalf or disclose same to any third party.

This non-compete agreement shall extend for a radius of _______ miles of Company's present location and shall be in full force and effect for ____ years, commencing with the date of employment termination.

This agreement shall be binding upon and inure to the benefit of the parties, their successors, assigns and personal representatives.

Officer ____

Company ____

Date ____

Employee ____

Date ____

Non-Disclosure and Confidentiality Agreement

FOR GOOD AND VALUABLE CONSIDERATION, receipt of which is hereby acknowledged by _______________________________ (Company), the undersigned employee hereby agrees and acknowledges:

That during the course of my employ there may be disclosed to me certain Company's trade secrets consisting but not limited to: technical information including methods, processes, formulae, compositions, systems, techniques, inventions, machines, computer programs and research projects and business information including customer lists, pricing data, sources of supply, financial data and marketing, production, or merchandising systems or plans.

I agree that I shall not during, or at any time after the termination of my employment with the Company, disclose or divulge to others including future employers, any trade secrets, confidential information, or any other proprietary data of the Company in violation of this agreement.

That upon the termination of my employment from the Company: I shall return to the Company all documents and property of the Company, including but not necessarily limited to: drawings, blueprints, reports, manuals, correspondence, customer lists, computer programs all other materials and all copies thereof relating in any way to the Company's business, or in any way obtained by me during the course of employ.

I further agree that I shall not retain copies, notes or abstracts of the foregoing.

The Company may notify any future or prospective employer or third party of the existence of this agreement and shall be entitled to full injunctive relief and any other legal remedies available for any breach.

This agreement shall be binding upon me and my personal representatives and successors in interest and shall inure to the benefit of the Company, its successors and assigns.

Signed this _______ day of _______________________, 20______.

______________________________   ______________________________
Company   Employee

Employment Agreement

This Agreement for Employment is made on this _____ day of ________, ___, by and between _________________________________, Employer and _________________________________, Employee.

The Employer shall employ Employee subject to the following terms and conditions.

1. Employment for the above Employee shall commence on ______________ (Date).

2. The following duties and responsibilities shall be competently performed by the Employee:

   In addition to the duties stated above, the Employee shall perform such further and other duties required by the Employer.

3. The Employee shall work ________ through ________ from _____ A.M. to _____ P.M. and such additional hours as are required by the Employer for the Employee to competently perform the duties of his position. The Employee shall use his or her best efforts on behalf of the Employer.

4. The Employee shall comply with all stated standards of performance, policies, rules and regulations. A company manual containing a more complete explanation of many of these standards has been given to the Employee. At this time, Employee acknowledges receipt of the company manual. The Employee shall also comply with such future Employer policies, rules, regulations, performance standards and manuals as may be published or amended from time to time.

5. The Employer shall make payment to the Employee a set amount as compensation for services rendered. The Employee agrees to accept the sum of ___________ ($______) per year, payable ____________ ______ in the amount of ____________ ($______). In addition to the above compensation, the Employee will be entitled to the following fringe benefits:

6. This contract of employment may terminate upon the occurrence of any of the following events: (a) the death of the Employee; (b) the failure of the Employee to perform his duties satisfactorily after notice

or warning thereof; (c) for just cause based upon nonperformance of duties by Employee; (d) economic reasons of the Employer which may arise during the term of this Agreement and which may be beyond the control of the Employer.

7. The Employee shall not, at any time during the period hereof for _____ years from the date of termination of this Agreement, directly or indirectly, within a geographic area of ______ miles, engage in, or become involved in any business competitive or similar to that of the Employer.

8. This Agreement may not be assigned without prior notice by either party. Such assignment is subject to the mutual consent and approval of any such assignment.

9. This Agreement constitutes the complete understanding between the parties, unless amended by a subsequent written instrument signed by the employer and employee. Any dispute under this contract shall be required to be resolved by binding arbitration of the parties hereto. Each party shall select one arbitrator and both arbitrators shall select a third. The arbitration shall be governed by the rules of the American Arbitration Association then in force and effect.

____

Employer's Signature

____

Employee's Signature

Request For Employment Reference

Date:

To:

From:

_______________________________ has applied to us seeking a position
as _____________________ names your company as a prior employer.

We are requesting a reference on the above applicant including the dates during which the applicant was employed by you, the date upon which the individual left your employment, a rating of his performance and the reason the individual left your employ.

Enclosed is a consent form executed by the above applicant.

____

Signature

Sales Representative Agreement

This agreement is made between ___________________________________
_______________________ (Company) and _______________________
_________________________________(Sales Representative).

Sales Representative agrees to:

1. Represent and sell the Company's ___________________________
   products / services in the geographic area of ___________________
   _________________________________.

2. Accurately represent and state Company policies to all potential and
   present customers.

3. Promptly mail in all leads and orders to the Company.

4. Inform the sales manager of all problems concerning Company
   customers within the sales territory.

5. Inform the sales manager if the Sales Representative is representing,
   or plans to represent any other business firm. In no event shall sales
   representative represent a competitive company or product line either
   within or outside the designated sales area.

6. Report to the Company with reasonable frequency to discuss sales
   activity within the territory.

7. Provide company with 30-days notice should the Representative
   intend to terminate this agreement.

8. Return promptly all materials and samples provided by the Company
   to the Representative if either party terminates this agreement.

The Company Agrees to:

1. Pay the following commissions to the Sales Representative:
   (a) ___________ percent of all prepaid sales, except as stated in (4)
   below.
   (b) ___________ percent of all credit sales, except as stated in (4) below.

2. To negotiate in advance of sale the commission percentage to be paid on all orders that the Company allows a quantity discount or other trade concession.

3. Commissions on refunds to customers or merchandise returned by the customer in which a commission has already been paid to the Representative shall be deducted from future commissions to be paid to the Representative by the Company.

4. Except by special arrangement, the following shall not be commissioned: ____

____

5. To provide the Sales Representative with reasonable quantities of business cards, brochures, catalogs and any product samples required for sales purposes.

6. To set minimum monthly quotas after consultation with the Sales Representative.

7. To grant Representative 30-days notice should the Company wish to terminate this agreement.

8. To pay commissions to the Representative on sales from existing customers for a period of ________________ months after this agreement is terminated by either party.

This constitutes the entire agreement.

This agreement shall be binding upon the parties and their successors and assigns.

Signed this ______ day of ________________ , ______.

____ Company

____ Sales Representative

A

accountability A responsibility imposed on a sales person for the success of a particular sales program. In general, an implicit requirement of a sales job-that the person given a job is responsible for making a success of that job and will be called on to justify performance.

Age Discrimination in Employment Act (ADEA) of 1967
A federal act that extends antidiscrimination protection to salespeople who are more than 40 years of age. In effect, the ADEA says an employer cannot discriminate against a potential sales person because of age if the person is otherwise capable of doing the job offered.

Americans with Disabilities Act (ADA) of 1990 The ADA is designed to provide job protection for handicapped individuals in private-sector companies with 15 or more employees who might be seeking employment in sales. That section of the act relevant to human resources is that it is illegal for an employer to discriminate against sales candidates otherwise qualified for a job solely because they are disabled. Reasonable accommodation is also mandated

applied rate The cost of a sales person's pay and benefits measured against how much a company is able to bill for goods or services sold by that employee.

area differential An allowance (i.e., higher pay or commissions for the same job) paid to salespeople who live in high-cost areas of the country (e.g., New York City as opposed to a small town in a rural area).

area wage survey A survey of what is being paid for particular sales positions in a particular area. Such a survey can be undertaken by individual companies. A more formal survey is published each year by the U.S. Bureau of Labor Statistics.

at-risk pay Any compensation that is not guaranteed (e.g., variable compensation, such as a sales person's commission or profit sharing for employees).

attention, interest, desire and action (AIDA) A four-step guide used by sales managers and human resources specialists when advertising job openings: (1) attract attention; (2) develop interest; (3) create desire; and (4) stimulate action.

B

background checks/checking The process by which an employer gathers information about a sales applicant from people familiar with that person in past situations-generally, education officials, previous employers and friends who provide references about character. The process can also involve checking credit history and court records. Information gathered in this way varies greatly in its accuracy and reliability.

benefits A generic term covering all compensation that is not strictly commissions, wages or salary (e.g., medical and dental insurance, financial assistance, 401(k) plans and profit sharing). Some benefits are government-mandated, such as unemployment compensation and workers' compensation. Employers generally agree that they can attract the best salespeople with attractive benefits packages. Benefits now account for more than one-third of the cost of employee compensation.

bona fide occupational qualification (BFOQ) Despite U.S. antidiscrimination laws, employers may discriminate on the basis of religion, age, national origin or sex if one or more or those characteristics is a BFOQ for that position. If previous sales experience is required, that is a BFOQ.

bonuses Cash payments to salespeople who achieve a certain sales or prospecting goal set by the sales manager. Bonuses are a form of variable compensation (i.e., they are not built into base salary but considered extra compensation).

buddy system A mentoring technique. A young sales person is assigned to a senior sales executive who in turn acts as the young sales person's coach and role model.

burnout Mental or physical fatigue on the job-to the extent that the sales person is no longer able to function adequately in that job. Although it can be caused by excessive stress at work, such as an unbearably heavy workload within a short deadline, it can also be caused by personal problems such as those of family or of finances.

C

career counseling Helping salespeople learn more about their own capabilities, limitations and objectives, including where they stand in an organization, what opportunities are available to them and what they will need in the way of training and experience to take advantage of those opportunities.

Civil Rights Act of 1964 Title VII of this act (as amended by the Equal Employment Opportunities Act of 1972 and the Civil Rights Act of 1991) forbids employer or union discrimination on the basis of race, color, religion, sex or national origin. Title VII also prohibits any kind of retaliation by an employer against any employee who brings a claim of discrimination against that employer.

coaching On-site training used to enhance the abilities and skills of entry-level sales trainees. A coach (who might be a supervisor but could also be a peer) sets goals that are difficult but can be attained, monitors the employee's attempt to reach those goals and provides feedback along the way. The advantage of coaching, besides this feedback, is that it enables salespeople to learn methods to improve their job performance and opens up lines of communication between various members of staff.

collaborative appraisal An evaluation of job performance involving the sales person and that employee's sales manager. They jointly establish the measures of performance, evaluate progress and together identify areas that should be improved.

commissions Incentive pay based on a percentage of the selling price of a product or service. Sales jobs are commonly, in part or total, compensated by commission-though some sales jobs do involve a base salary to which a commission is added, particularly in those sales jobs that involve a traditionally low-yield territory. Commissions are generally of two kinds: (1) a straight percentage commission of all sales; and (2) a commission that increases as a result of higher volume (e.g., 5 percent on sales of up to $500,000, 6 percent on sales beyond $500,000).

communication training That which is designed to improve the skills of sales and marketing personnel at all levels of an organization in transmitting and receiving information. It involves training in listening, speaking, reading and writing.

compensation The total package of rewards-pay, services, commissions benefits-offered to a sales person by the company. Any compensation package involves two components: (1) direct pay and (2) indirect pay, or benefits. A primary challenge to sales managers is mixing these components to attract the best employees.

conditions of employment Company policies and work rules that apply to salespeople and all employees (e.g., rules about tardiness, vacations, special circumstances, such as pregnancy). Often these conditions are codified in an employee handbook.

confidentiality agreement One signed by a sales person stipulating that he or she will not disclose company plans, designs, financial status or any other proprietary information that might be interesting to competitors-either during employment or after leaving the company.

Consolidated Omnibus Budget Reconciliation Act (COBRA) of 1985 COBRA requires group health plan providers to continue covering employees (usually for 18 months) in circumstances that would otherwise result in loss of coverage (e.g., when an employee has been terminated for reasons other than gross misconduct). Employers with fewer than 20 employees are exempt from COBRA's coverage; all other employers must continue to include the employee (and the employee's dependents, if they too were covered) in the group health plan, but the employee must pay the employer for the cost of coverage.

counter cyclical hiring A staffing strategy whereby companies recruit sales and marketing people, particularly managerial personnel, during economic downturns when more of such people are available. As opposed to hiring during economic upturns, when there is a demand, consequently a scarcity, of such key people. Those who practice counter cyclical hiring believe that they are creating a competitive advantage for themselves, as they will be staffed by highly competent people when there is an economic revival.

D

diversity In human resources, the concept that any company's workplace should include people of varying backgrounds, reflecting, if possible, the demographics of the area in which the company is located.

downsizing The planned (by management) elimination of jobs within a company or organization. This action may be driven by a simple attempt at cost-cutting (e.g., the company plans to eliminate a department, outsourcing its function to a vendor who promises to perform the department's functions at a lower cost to the company). More often, also driven by cost-costing but with a certain urgency involved, downsizing is a response to a downturn in the economy.

duty/duties The requirements of a job, comprised of a series of components. For example, a sales person provides direct contact with customers and potential customers–that is the sales person's duty.

E

early identification The recognition-by management or by the staff in a human resources department–that particular salespeople, though still at an early stage in their careers, have the potential to lead others, to manage, control and direct other people, in other words, are management material. A well-run company, having made this early identification, puts such people in jobs that will allow them to continue to develop these capabilities.

employee code of conduct Increasingly, companies issue their employees a formal (written) list of types of behavior that are (or are not) acceptable within the workplace. Topics that are usually covered include appropriate behavior to the company's customers and to coworkers; rules about violence in the workplace; the company's policy on discrimination; and the kinds of discipline to which the company will resort if its rules are now followed.

employee handbook As companies grow, management no longer has constant contact with salespeople and other employees, they often decide to issue a manual that describes such things as company products, human resource policies, employee benefits and work standards. Most companies feel that issuing such an employee handbook contributes to workplace morale because expectations and policies are clear. The only downside to such a document is that it is often interpreted as a kind of contract (employers must be clear to note at the beginning of the handbook that it is not in any way a contract).

Employee Retirement Income Security Act (ERISA) of 1974 The law by which the federal government regulates employee pension plans. ERISA has no power to force employers to provide pensions for employees, but, if an employer does offer a pension plan, virtually all aspects of that pension plan's practices are governed by ERISA.

employment contract A document that sets out the terms and conditions of the employment relationship between a sales person and his or her employer.

employment interview A conversation initiated by a potential employer with a job applicant for a particular job. The purpose of this conversation is to determine whether the applicant has suitable professional and personal skills to do the job well. Although background checks and references are, for most companies, a crucial part of the decision to hire a new employee, most sales managers would agree that the employment interview is still the primary determining factor in hiring a new employee.

employment at will The agreement between employer and employee that provides freedom of action–the employee may leave a job at any time and for whatever reason (usually, though, the employee is asked to give appropriate notice); likewise, the employer can terminate the employee at any time and for any reason. Although this agreement is almost universally assumed in any employment arrangement, it is best for both parties if this agreement is put in writing (e.g., in an employment contract). If the at-will concept is unacceptable to one or more of the parties–if, for example, an employer is willing to give the employee a cash settlement if the employee will give 6 months notice–this kind of variant should be stated in the employment contract.

Equal Employment Opportunity Commission (EEOC) The federal agency that administers Title VII of the Civil Rights Act (as well as the Equal Pay Act, the Pregnancy Discrimination Act, the Age Discrimination Act and the Americans with Disabilities Act). This agency processes charges of discrimination against people covered by these various acts and works to achieve resolution through conciliation or legal action.

Equal Pay Act of 1963 This act requires employers to give women pay equal to men if both are performing work of similar skill and responsibility. The act does not apply if there are issues of seniority or performance involved or any other factor unrelated to gender.

F

fair employment practices law All federal or local laws that guarantee the rights of employees (e.g., the Age Discrimination Act or the Pregnancy Discrimination Act).

Fair Labor Standards Act (FLSA) of 1938 A law that mandates certain basic requirements of the U.S. workplace having to do with (1) minimum wage; (2) overtime pay; (3) equal pay; (4) record-keeping requirements; and (5) child labor laws. Only certain professional and administrative employees are exempt from FLSA provisions.

Family and Medical Leave Act of 1993 A federal law mandating that employers must provide unpaid leaves of absence of up to 12 weeks for employees for childbirth, the care of seriously ill children or other family members, or for the illness of employees themselves. During such leaves, the employee's medical benefits continue in force and, on returning, the employee must be given the same (or an equivalent) position in the company with no forfeiture of benefits.

401(k) plans Named for that section of the 1978 Revenue Act that authorizes them, 401(k) plans allow an employer, at the direction of the employee, to reduce an employee's taxable salary by a particular amount, adding an employer contribution and then depositing those funds (the employee's and employer's contribution) into an investment fund for the employee's retirement.

glass ceiling A slang term originally used to describe the phenomenon whereby women would rise to certain positions in companies, as a result of their abilities, then be unable to rise any further, despite their qualifications to do so-a phenomenon that is the result of gender prejudice.

H

halo effect The practice of giving a favorable rating about a particular sales person because one outstanding characteristic causes the rater to underestimate that person's bad qualities.

human resource management The need for companies/organizations to manage employees in a manner likely to promote a strategic business or social objective.

I

incentive plan A plan that provides financial rewards to employees whose productivity exceeds a predetermined standard.

independent contractors Self-employed salespeople who work for an individual client or for a company. They are used by companies for specialized tasks or, more frequently, for adding staff during periods of high demand or for managing territories where it is not cost effective to have an in-house representative available.

integrity testing Tests administered (primarily) to new sales applicants to determine whether they are likely to be to be guilty, if hired, of bad work behavior-generally, whether they will be honest and diligent. Although such tests are widely administered, there is a great deal of disagreement among sales professionals and human resource personnel about their ultimate value.

J

job description A written summary of the nature of a sales position, including such elements as job title, mission/purpose of the job, primary tasks involved, guidelines and controls (e.g., purpose of supervisor), required knowledge and skills and a description of the work environment. A job description does not necessarily include compensation information.

job enrichment An attempt to redesign jobs (usually to make them more interesting or more challenging) to motivate people to sell to their full capacity and ability and improve employee morale, job satisfaction and commitment to the organization.

job evaluation A process designed to help in establishing pay differentials across jobs within a single company; the evaluation focuses on job complexity, skills required and value to the company.

job performance How well a person does a job and how much that employee contributes to a company's success. Job performance is a central concern of sales managers, not least because it is a measure of success in the hiring process.

job stress The mental or physical pressures of a job. Some stress can motivate a sales person to try harder, provided it is not too intense. Often, however, job stress can cause an employee to perform less well, particularly if the stress is overwhelming, leading to burnout and possibly resignation.

just cause A legal term used in connection with the termination of a sales person, meaning that the employer used every recourse to avoid termination but in the end had no other choice. The seven tests for just cause include relevant reasonableness, adequate notice, investigation, fairness, adequacy of proof, equal treatment and appropriate penalty.

M

management audit A detailed analysis of the quality of the performance of sales or other managers in any organization and how well they perform in tasks involving planning, organizing, staffing, directing and controlling.

management by objectives (MBO) A management technique whereby an employer, working together with a sales employee, identifies certain job goals for the employee, discusses the ways in which these goals can be achieved and then together monitor the accomplishment of those goals.

mentoring programs Any training in which experienced members of the sales staff instruct and guide newer members in acquiring particular job skills.

merit pay Increases in compensation that are based on a performance appraisal (i.e., how well someone is doing a job as opposed to other factors, such as length of service with the company or a union-mandated wage hike).

motivation A goal-directed stimulus. Personal drives (needs, wants and desires) for certain goals as a result of reinforcement from the organization in the form of incentives, encouragement, feedback or rewards.

multiple cutoff selection procedures The practice of removing a sales applicant from consideration for a job if that applicant falls below the expected level of attainment on one or more selection criteria.

N

negotiation biases Lapses from rational thought or behavior that can occur during employment discussions or sales presentations when negotiators are too committed to their own points of view.

new employee orientation The planned introduction-via previously determined methods-of new salespeople to their jobs, coworkers and the policies and expectations of the company for which they will be working.

noncompete agreements An employer who employs an individual with particular skills, training or knowledge (or the sales person who gains specialist knowledge by working for the employer) may ask her to sign an agreement stating that, if that she leaves the company, the employee will not work for a competitor for a specified period of time. Noncompete agreements that attempt to prevent an employee from future work in his profession are usually nonenforceable for the reason that courts view them as unreasonable.

nonstandardized interview An interview in which the sales candidate is encouraged to speak candidly and freely about any subject. There is no attempt by the interviewer to gather predetermined information from the applicant or to direct the conversation.

O

on-the-job training (OJT) Assigning sales trainees to particular jobs and asking them to observe and learn from the sales manager or regional manager or employees already doing those jobs. The advantages are its low cost and the opportunities it provides for interaction between trained employees and newcomers. Its disadvantage is that some employees are reluctant to take time away from their own job to help a new salespeople.

organizational culture The practices, but more the spirit, of a particular company. It is believed to come from two sources: (1) the policies and goals of management; and (2) the behavior of employees in supporting company strategies.

P

pay for performance A form of compensation linked to an individual's skill at a particular job. The sales manager sets performance criteria for the salespeople and base compensation on whether these criteria have been met.

pay satisfaction The positive or negative feelings an employee has about the compensation she receives for a job.

performance appraisal Identifying, observing, measuring and developing human performance in companies/organizations.

Pregnancy Discrimination Act (PDA) of 1978 An amendment to Title VII of the Civil Rights Act of 1964 that states that sexual discrimination also includes discrimination as a result of pregnancy and childbirth. In effect, women cannot be subjected to adverse treatment because of pregnancy.

Privacy Act of 1974 A law that holds that any disclosure of private information without the consent of the individual is an invasion of privacy. The purpose of the act is to protect the privacy of persons employed by the U.S. government.

R

recruiting The activities that produce a group of applicants for a particular sales job. Good recruiting involves planning a series of activities (e.g., advertisements for the job, job postings within the company and writing job descriptions) as well as a willingness to learn from past mistakes.

recruiting sources Those means used by companies/organizations to bring job openings to the attention of potential sales candidates. They are of two types, internal and external. Internal refers to methods that transmit information to current employees (e.g., job postings). External refers to any methods directed to individuals who are not current employees (e.g., advertisements in professional journals or in local newspapers).

reference checks A component of background checking whereby an employer verifies information on a potential sales employee's application (e.g., about schooling and previous employment). Many companies also ask applicants for references that will verify character.

Rehabilitation Act of 1973 A law protecting handicapped workers employed by or looking for jobs with government contractors and/or government-financed organizations from discrimination. Handicapped persons in the private sector are covered by the Americans with Disabilities Act of 1990. Title VII of the Civil Rights Act of 1964 does not cover discrimination against handicapped workers.

remedial training Repeat training or guided practice to correct deficiencies in an sales employee's job performance.

S

sales force compensation The financial and nonfinancial rewards given to salespeople as a result of their success in selling potential customers the company's goods or services. Compensation often consists of a base salary plus an incentive bonus, such as a commission.

search firms Also called headhunters. An organization, working on a retainer from an employer, that searches for qualified sales candidates for key openings. Search firms often also recommend compensation packages.

self-awareness training Training in which a sales trainee completes and analyzes one or more self-assessment exercises, then receives feedback from others-usually a supervisor.

sexual harassment A form of sex discrimination that is precisely defined by the Equal Employment Opportunity Commission. Unwanted and persistent sexual advances (and requests for sexual favors) constitute harassment when (1) submission is made a condition of employment; (2) rejection affects the way in which the employee is treated in the future; or (3) the conduct has the effect of interfering with the employee's work performance and/or of creating a hostile workplace environment. Employers can be held legally responsible for allowing this kind of sexual harassment to take place.

situational interview An interview in which a sales applicant is asked how he or she would react when faced with a hypothetical problem in a job situation. If well chosen, these problems and how they are resolved by the applicant can provide insight into the applicant's personality and the success that applicant is likely to have on the job.

T

team-building training A process whereby the sales team members analyze the ways in which they work together and devise strategies for becoming more effective.

team-based incentives Financial rewards for sales employees (and others) based on the performance of the group within the company to which they belong. Such incentives are thought to foster common goals and objectives, encouraging members of the group to collaborate more closely to achieve those goals.

turnover The change in the composition of a particular work force as a result of termination, resignation or retirement. The sales manager's challenge involves buttressing employee morale, developing active policies of recruitment (so there is always a new employee pool) and monitoring hiring and training costs.

V, W

variable compensation Pay that varies according to specified criteria (e.g., incentive pay or merit pay). Compensation that is not a part of an employee's base pay.

veteran status A protected category under federal antidiscrimination statutes. For instance, the Veterans Re-Employment Rights Act of 1974 mandates that an employee called to active service must be released from employment by his or her employer and be allowed to return to the same job (when service is complete) with no reduction in status or pay. This right lasts for as long as the employee is a member of the U.S. Armed Services.

wrongful discharge Unfair termination of a sales employee by an employer, usually defined as of one of three types: (1) breach of contract; (2) violation of generally accepted employee practices; or (3) an action that most people would agree is unjust (e.g., an employee fired vindictively following a heated argument with a manager).

Index

Q

qualifying 28, 87, 107, 108, 114
quota 1, 6, 25, 26, 40, 41, 66, 120, 135

R

ratio 39, 40, 49, 57, 106
reasonable accommodation 16
records
    academic 6
    criminal 6, 7
    driving 6
    keeping 37
    public 6
recruiting
    ads 2, 8
    national agencies 123
references 4, 7, 35, 91, 138, 141, 146
Request For Employment Reference (form)
    133
retaining 1
role-playing
    team 33
    true 32
rookies 35, 49

S

Sales Company, The 123
Salesforce.com 123
Sales Representative Agreement (form) 134
Schneider Sales Management, Inc. 124
screening 8, 9
search engines 8
self-image 75, 76, 80, 83, 84
selling
    balanced 26
    long-term 23
    short-term 23, 24
services ii, 4, 23, 25, 26, 43, 57, 61, 70,
    87, 99, 114, 123, 124, 125, 131, 134,
    137, 140, 147
slump 68, 70, 74, 81, 82
square peg 19, 20

survey 5, 9, 26, 27, 30, 34, 39, 71, 108,
    109, 119, 124, 138

T

target 1, 2, 8, 41, 71, 78, 79, 80, 91, 102,
    105, 124
team 1, 2, 5, 7, 17, 28, 33, 38, 43, 50, 54,
    62, 65, 66, 67, 68, 88, 89, 93, 147
telemarketing 15, 36
territory 3, 4, 14, 23, 25, 26, 41, 50, 57,
    67, 89, 92, 105, 106, 107, 113, 123,
    134, 139
Topline Leadership, Inc. 124
trade show 42, 43, 44
training vii, 1, 11, 12, 22, 27, 28, 29, 30,
    31, 32, 33, 34, 41, 42, 43, 48, 49, 58,
    65, 67, 68, 73, 83, 88, 90, 91, 95,
    108, 111, 112, 120, 123, 124, 125,
    139, 144, 145, 146, 147
turnover 7, 94, 107, 147

V

Vanguard Sales Manager 123
veterans 50, 67, 148

Smart, Friendly and Informative

The 50 plus one series from Encouragement Press are thorough and detailed guides covering a wide range of topics–both personal and business related, supplying you, the reader, the information and resources you need and want in an easy-to-read format.

50 plus one Questions When Buying a Car
by Stephen Edwards

50 plus one Questions When Buying a Car is the perfect self-help guide for every potential car buyer, whether you are buying new or pre-owned vehicles. How do you tell if a used car was in an accident? What features on a new car provide good values? What is the best way to finance a car? This book could save you hundreds or thousands of dollars over the many cars you will buy in your lifetime.

224 pgs
ISBN-13: 978-1-933766-05-8

$14.95 U.S.
$19.95 CAN

50 plus one Tips to Building a Retirement Nest Egg
by Linda M. Magoon & Poonum Vasishth

50 plus one Tips to Building a Retirement Nest Egg shows you how in concise, understandable and practical language how to prepare for your financial future. You do not need a financial planner or stockbroker to get started. All you need is the will to turn around your financial well-being and the help tips this book offers.

224 pgs
ISBN-13: 978-1-933766-02-7

$14.95 U.S.
$19.95 CAN

50 plus one Tips to Preventing Identity Theft
by Elizabeth Drake

50 plus one Tips to Preventing Identity Theft is your first step to protecting your family, your money and your identity. This book is particularly important if you travel internationally or buy on the Internet. The more complicated your financial life, the more vulnerable you may be and the more important this book is to keeping your finances secure.

224 pgs
ISBN-13: 978-1-933766-06-5

$14.95 U.S.
$19.95 CAN

50 plus one Tips When Hiring & Firing Employees
Edited by Linda M. Magoon & Donna de St. Aubin

Hiring a new employee is one of the most important and time-consuming tasks a manager or entrepreneur can undertake. Firing an employee is an emotionally draining and difficult action, no matter the length of service or level of responsibility. *50 plus one Tips When Hiring & Firing Employees* shows you how to hire the right people for the job and fire those who do not work out, and avoid litigation.

224 pgs
ISBN-13: 978-1-933766-03-4

$14.95 U.S.
$19.95 CAN

To learn more about books of interest from Encouragement Press, or to order visit

www.encouragementpress.com or call 1.253.303.0033